# God's Blueprint for Planet Earth

## The Book of Revelation Explained

## Dr. Ray W. Yerbury

D.B.S., M.A., B.Th., B.Ecom., Dip.Ind. Chem., C.Chem.
F.R.A.C.I., F.A.I.M., F.G.A.A., A.(Aust).I.M.M., F.A.I.Pet.

ii

Typeset by : Cross Publications (Pagemaker 3)
Printed by :  Queensland Binding Services

# Acknowledgment

I am ever grateful to the many Christian friends who have encouraged me over the past years to write a systematic and an easy readable analysis of the Book of Revelation. What follows is a result of 25 years of consistent study and research in the prophetic area of God's Holy Word.

Once again my mentor and friend, Dr. Clifford Wilson has given expert advise in the area of style and grammar. The painstaking proof-reading of this manuscript involved many hours of sacrifice. For this I am most grateful.

---

*This book is dedicated to all the*
**Young People and Adults of
Stafford North Baptist Church**
Brisbane, Queensland, Aust.

*who have sat under my teaching over many years.*

# CONTENTS

# Preface

The year 1991 was indeed a momentous one. Newspaper headlines around the world carried daily reports of human problems and tragedies. Wars; Revolutions; Drought; Hunger; Hurricanes; Earthquakes; Terrorism; Illegal drugs; Robberies; Murders.  News has become almost synonymous with "bad news."

But there is "good news." The prophets of the Bible foretold of a time when a utopian condition would exist on planet earth. A time when there would be a food surplus and farmers will prosper. A world where people will learn to live without religious and racial hatred. A world where people will learn to respect the cultures, abilities and talents of one another. A time of mutual understanding and universal love.

Impossible I hear you say?  No.  Indeed such a world will be a reality. The Bible foretells major events about God's plan for this earth, including the future of the human race and how God's government will replace the present system of a human-ruled society.

The Book of Revelation is the only book of the Bible that unveils important future events on God's calendar relative to the purpose for the human race. In addition we can also see how Scripture in other parts of the Bible fill in details concerning many related events yet to take place.

The ultimate aim of all believers is to spend Eternity with Jesus Christ the Son and God the Father. The world leaders on the one hand promise *a new world order* and a hope that such global changes will precipitate a political stability that in turn will enable worldwide peace to be realized in our time. In reality, however, all they can deliver is a false hope to a world gone mad.

On the other hand, God has promised that *a new world order* will one day emerge - a time when world peace, prosperity, and plenty will fill the earth; a time when wars, famines, floods, disease, and corruption will be things of the past. This promise of the "Blessed Hope" for the believer and the Second Coming of Jesus Christ to this earth to reign with His saints for a thousand years ( referred to by Bible students as the Millennium), is one of the great certainties and hope for this age.

One of the great lies perpertrated by Satan is that Heaven and Hell do not exist. This is a belief of the New Age Movement. But the Bible attests to a physical Heaven and Hell. The Book of Revelation is mostly concerned about a judgment to Eternal life (a new Earth and Heavens), and a judgment to Eternal damnation (Hell and the Lake of Fire).

Most people don't like to think of the existence of a Hell and we don't hear much about Heaven these days. The reason for this is quite simple. For over a generation now, we have been occupied with being well-adjusted people in the here and now and enjoying our affluence - a sort of *Heaven on earth* mentality. Even much of our prophetic teaching and preaching, while delving into areas important to interpreting end-time events, seems to stop short of moving into the realm of the glory that is to follow.

The desperate need in our evangelical churches today is a revival among Christians of the teaching related to the covenants. We ignore the blessings promised to God's chosen people - the Jews. We have lost Abraham's desire to look "....... for a city with foundations, whose architect and builder is God" (Heb.11:10). In fact, we even fail to realize the significance of the promises given by Jesus to His bride - the Church. The perpetual "Maranatha" (O Lord come) greetings of the early believers, in anticipation of the Lord's coming and the promise of a Heaven, is virtually extinct nowadays.

The main purpose of this book is to show in the clearest way possible that the Book of Revelation, from Chapter four to the end, is a sequence of future events on God's Eternal calendar. Every activity has a definite pattern and purpose. All events lead people into a decision making process. The end result is either a dwelling place in the "Lake of Fire," or the blessing of Eternity with the Creator in the new Jerusalem, which will comes down to "the New Earth."

The book has been written from the viewpoint of the pretribulation and premillennial scheme of events. Because it is primarily concerned with an analysis of the sequence of future events, the author has chosen not to analyse in any detail the various other viewpoints as briefly mentioned in Chapter 1.

It is my prayer that each reader will seek wisdom and clear understanding from the Holy Spirit as he or she continues to diligently search the Scriptures for a "more sure word of prophecy" (2 Peter 1:19).

May God bless all who read this book in conjunction with the Word of God.

Ray W. Yerbury
Brisbane, Queensland
December 1st, 1991

**Map 1**

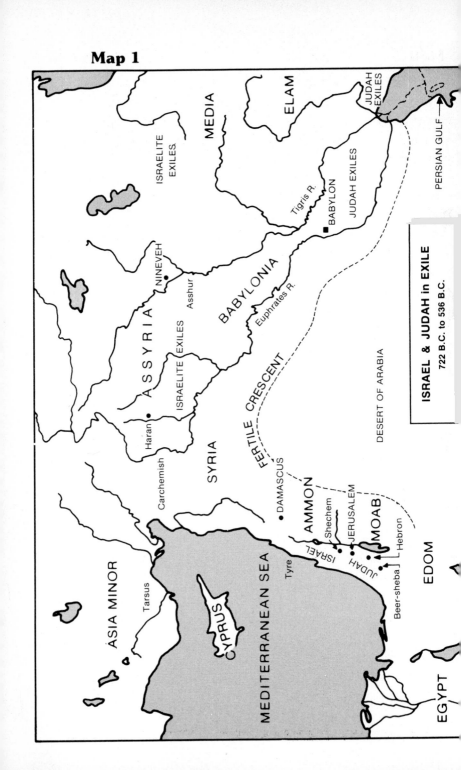

ISRAEL & JUDAH in EXILE
722 B.C. to 536 B.C.

**Map 2**

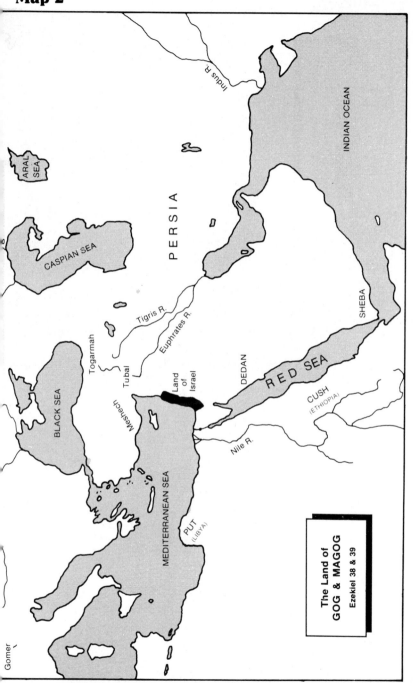

The Land of
GOG & MAGOG
Ezekiel 38 & 39

# Map 3

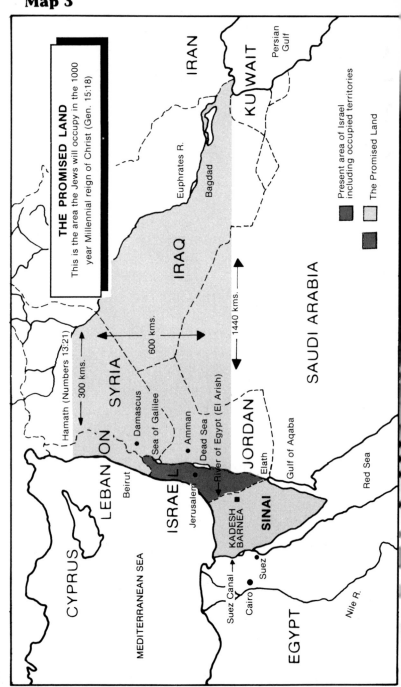

**THE PROMISED LAND**
This is the area the Jews will occupy in the 1000 year Millennial reign of Christ (Gen. 15:18)

Present area of Israel including occupied territories

The Promised Land

# Chapter 1

---

# The Background and Outline to the Book of Revelation

The book of Revelation has been viewed by many as a book of mystery. They have assumed it is beyond understanding and so have ignored its teachings. Many well respected Pastors and Bible teachers have begun at the book of Genesis, only to arrive at the book of Jude and return to the beginning without even a comment on the only book in the Scriptures that promises a blessing to its readers.

The book of Revelation has also been called "The Apocalypse" and this term has fascinated the western world more than any other part of the Bible. Many stories, plays, and movie films have been based on familiar expressions which emanate from the last book of the New Testament: The Four Horsemen, The Mark of the Beast- 666, Babylon the Great, The Lake of Fire, Armageddon, The Millennium, just to name a few.

The expression "Apocalypse" is a transliteration of the Greek word *"apokalypsis."* It means an "unveiling," "disclosure," "revelation," as with the revealing of something hidden behind a curtain or cover. Thus the book is an unveiling of that which otherwise could not be known.

The title of this book in the Greek text is *Apokalypsis Ioannou,* "Revelation of John." A better title comes from the first verse: *Apokalypsis Iesou Christoue,* "Revelation of Jesus Christ." This could mean either a revelation which came from Christ, or a revelation which is about Christ - both are appropiate. Because of the unified contents of this book, it should not, as is often the case, be called "Revelations."

### We Live In Momentous Days

For almost 2000 years, readers could be forgiven for thinking that the imagery and visions of Revelation predicting worldwide destruction and death seemed quite bizarre. That's hardly true today. This sleepy, comparatively quiet planet has suddenly erupted in world-shaking violence, beginning with World War 1 in 1914. But we have seen nothing yet compared with what is soon to come. Even the events of the 1991 Gulf War, together with the disturbances in Russia and the Baltic States will pale into insignificance when compared to the judgments as detailed in God's blueprint for a sinful and degenerate society.

For most people, however, the book will always remain a mystery, especially to those who haven't had the opportunity to study the Bible. For Christians, it is one of the least read and, to some extent, the most difficult to understand. One commentary says: "...... For the most part modern readers find the book unintelligible. This is largely because it abounds in symbolism of a type that we do not use and to which we no longer possess the key. Yet this kind of imagery was readily comprehensible to the men of the day. Indeed, this partly accounts for our difficulties." [1]

## A Third of the Bible is Prophecy

Approximately one third of all the Bible is devoted to prophecy. Many of the books in the Old Testament—Isaiah, Jeremiah, Ezekiel, Daniel, and all the so-called "minor prophets" are devoted almost exclusively to prophecy (recognizing that "prophecy" has two aspects - **i. foretelling** future events and **ii. forthtelling** the mind and will of God for the present generation).

But the actual framework or superstructure of all the prophecies can be found in just two prophetic books, one in the Old, and the other in the New Testament - the Books of Daniel and Revelation.

While the Book of Revelation itself is a vital key to a large portion of the other prophecies spread throughout the Bible, there are certain **KEYS** which unlock this book to understanding.

One very important key is that the reader or student of prophecy should have at least a rudimentary understanding of Hebrew customs. This in itself implies a good working knowledge of the Old Testament.

A further key to understanding the Book of Revelation is that events are generally unfolding sequentially - i.e., one future event is followed by another in an orderly manner. But there are also a number of events that occur simultaneously. Thus the four horsemen judgments of chapter 6 take place throughout the seven years of Tribulation and not just at any one point in time.

A final key is that the Book of Revelation is really a story-flow, relating one future event to another in a definite time sequence, with the occasional inserts injected into the continuous story-thread.

With this brief background, let us now draw back the curtain on the future. Many books have been written on this subject. This is not just another commentary on Revelation as such, but rather it is a journey into the future where God is the audience and the people of the world are the actors. The stage is set both in Heaven and on Planet Earth.

The drama is in three parts:

**Act 1. The Seven Year Tribulation Period**
**Act 2. The Thousand Year Reign of Christ**
**Act 3. The Eternal Reign of God the Father**

### The Scribe of Revelation

The author of the Book of Revelation is none other than Jesus Christ. However, the scribe introduces himself simply as John. Early traditions unanimously declared that Revelation was written by the apostle John. This book is generally accepted as the last New Testament book, and was probably written during the latter part of the Roman Emperor

Domitian's reign (A.D. 81-96).

John was an elderly man banished to the Greek island of Patmos, either by force or choice. He was there, "... *because of the word of God and the testimony of Jesus Christ*" (Rev.1:9). It is noteworthy that even at the venerable age of the nineties, John refused to compromise his faithful preaching concerning the resurrected, glorified, and coming Redeemer.

Patmos is a rocky, wind-swept, 26 square kilometer island in the southern Aegean Sea, about 50 kilometers off the coast of modern day Turkey. It was a Roman penal colony to which authorities sent political offenders. While imprisoned on the island, John had an amazing encounter of the Heavenly kind.

## Apocalypse Now

The Book of Revelation can be likened to the script for a full length feature film about the future. John is simply the scribe or secretary writing down the details of the movie's script, which he receives by way of a vision. Yet he is not simply taking dictation. The word of God says, "*who testifies to everything he saw* ." In other words he was an eyewitness to everything he wrote, using his own familiar language of the day, his experiences, and his feelings. Revelation then is a book of visions, imparted through the mind of a man chosen by God, and moved by the Spirit for this monumentally important task of unveiling the future  plans of Jesus Christ for Planet Earth.

The readers of the words of this prophecy should then see themselves as part of the events unfolding in the  book. Whether their abode is to be in the Heavenly realm, or whether they remain on *terra- firma*, will primarily be determined by their relationship to Jesus Christ.

## The Message is Urgent

It is usual in the summary of a book to emphasize a certain required action, but this is not so with Revelation. This book from the beginning continually prods the reader to view the events described in its pages as imminent. For example:

**Verse 1:** "*The revelation of Jesus Christ, which God gave him to show his servants what must **soon take place**.*"

**Verse 3:** *"Blessed is the one who reads the words of this prophecy, and blessed are those who hear it and take to heart what is written in it, because the time is near."*

John records in chapter 10:6 the words of an angel who announces that the final events of the Lord's day should begin. *"... There will be no more delay."*

Many episodes described in the book are often written as though the reader is an eye-witness to what has already begun to happen. *"And there was war in Heaven"* (Rev.12:7); *"... the devil has gone down to you"* (Rev.12:12); *"... the hour of judgment has come"* (Rev.14:7); *"... fallen fallen is Babylon the Great"* (Rev.14:8).

The urgency of Christ's message is most pronounced in the final chapter. He is admonishing the reader to consider the events described in Revelation as those which are imminent (Rev.22:6). Furthermore, it is clear that the words of the book are not to be sealed from view, *"because the time is near"* (verse 10). Jesus is saying, *"Behold, I am coming soon! My reward is with me, and I will give to everyone according to what he has done "*(verse 12).

The gracious and loving nature of our Lord, who desires that none should perish, is clearly demonstrated in the second last verse of the Bible: *"He who testifies to these things says, 'Yes I am coming soon' "* (verse 20).

A sense of moral urgency underscores the Apocalypse. Time, or the passing of time, is very brief. We see events occurring in the world that are rapidly moving to a climax before the church is to be glorified. But events will reach crisis point just before the physical return of Jesus Christ with his saints to the earth. The only way to find safety from God's wrath in this life and perfect salvation in the next is to confess our sins and to step out in faith and believe in the Lord Jesus Christ (Rev.3:10).

## Chapter Outline of Revelation

1. John's introduction. Christ establishes His Deity.
2&3. The messages or letters to the seven churches.
4. The Throne in Heaven.
5. The title deed to Earth. The Lamb of God.
6. The six seal judgments. The four horsemen.
7. The multitude of saved people during the Tribulation.
8. The four trumpet plagues of the seventh seal.
9. The fifth and sixth trumpet plagues.
10. The prelude to God's wrath.
11. The two super-witnesses. The seventh trumpet sounded.
12. Satan's exit from Heaven. Persecution of Israel.
13. The two Beasts - Antichrist and the False Prophet.
14. The Rapture of the 144,000. The gospel proclaimed by an Angel. The mid-point of the Tribulation.
15. The seven Angels with seven plagues.
16. The seven bowls (vials) of God's wrath.
17. The false church of the Tribulation period.
18. The fall of the world's political and economic systems-Babylon the Great.
19. The Marriage Supper of the Lamb. The Second Coming of Jesus Christ.
20. The Millennial (1000 years) Reign of Jesus Christ. Satan judged. The Great White Throne Judgment.
21. The new Jerusalem.
22. The new Heavens and the new Earth. The Eternal Reign of God the Father.

# SYNOPSIS OF THE BOOK OF REVELATION

### GRACE
**Ch.1    Chs. 2&3**

—Past—  —Present—    ... Chs. 4 to 18 .................    ... Chs. 19 to 22 ...

### GOVERNMENT

### GLORY

**Christ in Beginning**    **Christ in the Midst**

Chs.1-3 The Witness of the Lamb Instructed

Church on the Earth

------- Future -------

**Christ on the Throne**

Chs. 4-5:   Worship of the Lamb Invited
Chs. 6-19:  Wrath of the Lamb Invoked
Ch. 20:    Reign of the Lamb Instituted
Chs. 21-22: The Wife of the Lamb Introduced

Chs.4 to 18  -  Saints in Glory
Ch.19        -  Saints on planet Earth
Ch.20        -  Saints reigning with Christ  { Wedlock of the Lamb
Chs.21 to 22 -  Saints on the New Earth with New Heavens

Ch. 19- The Return of Jesus Christ
Ch. 20- The Millennial Reign of Christ
Chs. 21-22 - The New Heavens & the New Earth

Ch. 1       - Christ establishes His Deity
Chs. 2 & 3  - The Letters to the Seven Churches
Chs. 4 & 5  - The Thrones in Heaven
Chs. 6 - 8  - The Seal Judgments
Chs. 8- 10  - The Trumpet Judgments
Chs.11- 14  - Conflict of Good  vs Evil
Chs. 15-16  - The Vial/Bowl Judgments
Chs. 17-18  - The Fall of World Government & Religion

# Definition of Terms

Before proceeding, it is important to define some basic terms we will encounter on our journey in life's end-time drama.

**1. The Rapture:** This refers to the "catching away" of the church - the redeemed from this world by Christ just prior to the beginning of the Tribulation period.

**2. The Great Tribulation:** That period of seven years when God will smelt the hardened heart of the Jews, while at the same time He will judge the world at large for its current and past sins.

**3. The Judgment Seat of Christ:** Also referred to as the "bema judgment". This is the place where Christ will judge all Christians on the basis of their discipleship. This event will take place in Heaven.

**4. The Marriage Supper of the Lamb:** This event is to take place in Heaven, probably sometime during the last three and one half years of the Tribulation period. The occasion will unite the Jews and Gentiles into one body called Saints.

**5. The Revelation of Jesus Christ:** This term is also commonly referred to as the Second Coming (Advent) of Jesus Christ. Christ will return to this earth with His saints to judge the nations (Matt.25:31-46), and to set up His Millennial Reign from Jerusalem.

**6. The Battle of Armageddon:** The last great battle culminating in the return of Jesus Christ. It will be led by the forces of the Antichrist and will be fought on Israel's soil in two major locations:

**a)** At the historical battle scene of Megiddo to the north of Jerusalem.

**b)** In the valley of Jehoshaphat (Joel 3:2), which many believe is the valley separating the Mount of Olives and the Temple Mount in Jerusalem.

**7. The Millennium:** This is the period of one thousand years, beginning 30 days after the judgment of the Nations ( Dan. 12:11). At this time Jesus Christ will rule in perfect righteousness and peace over the state of Israel in particular and the world in general.

**8. The Judgment of the Nations:** This is also referred to as the "sheep and goat judgment." After Israel is delivered from the Antichrist, Jesus Christ will determine those who will be permitted to enter the Millennial Kingdom. The criteria for judgment will be personal righteousness as believers in Christ, and/or their attitude to God's chosen people the Jews during the Great Tribulation.

**9. The Great White Throne Judgment:** This is the final judgment following the Millennium. All the unsaved of all ages will receive their sentence of eternal damnation to be spent in the "Lake of Fire" for Eternity.

**10. The Premillennial View:** There will be a literal, earthly 1000 year reign of Jesus Christ, which has been preceded by the Rapture. (This is the view of the author.)

**11. The Postmillennial View:** There is to be a literal Millennium on this earth as the result of an evangelistic thrust to spread the gospel, resulting in vast numbers of people accepting salvation. Christ will return to earth at its conclusion.

**12. The Amillennial View:** Holders of this view deny the existence of a literal Millennium. They say there is no future for Israel, and all the prophecies of the Old Testament are to be spiritually realized in the church.

**13. The Pretribulation View:** This is the view held by a large number of Christians. The Rapture of the church will not only be premillennial but pretribulational: i.e.,the church will not experience the severe period of suffering of the Tribulation.

**14. The Posttribulational View:** They agree with the pretribulational view that the Rapture will be premillennial, but hold that it will occur *after* the Great Tribulation: i.e., the church will be on earth during the seven year period.

**15. The Midtribulation View:** People of this view also agree that the Rapture will be premillennial, but say that it will occur at the midpoint of the great Tribulation: i.e., the church will only experience the first half ( $3\frac{1}{2}$ years) of the Tribulation. They will escape the period of severe suffering.

**Notes:**

1. New Bible Dictionary- 2nd ed, pp. 1027 ff, article entitled **Revelation**, Book of.

# Chapter 2

---

# The Seven Churches in Prophecy

The very purpose of the book of Revelation is to show people of this generation the coming world-shaking events of "The Day of the Lord." This is the time of God's judgments, leading up to and climaxing in the Second Coming of Christ.

In the first chapter of Revelation we are introduced to the principal actor, the "*Alpha and the Omega, the one who is, who was, and who is to come, the Almighty.*" He is also revealed as the one who, in His glorified state, is in the midst of the churches. So it is therefore natural that he should have a message not only to the select number of churches of John's day, but also to the church universal- the church of all believers through all ages.

The vision that John received while on the island of Patmos emphasizes beyond doubt just who is the true spiritual leader of the church.

The first real message of the book is contained in the second and third chapters - the messages to the seven churches in Asia Minor, which today is in western Turkey. There is a common theme associated with each of the letters. If God's people did not repent of their sins, God would remove His power from their midst.

John warned the people that the candlestick (the churches) might be removed, and the casual tourist and student of Biblical history finds that this is exactly what has happened. Today these once proud cities are in ruins, amidst a Muslim dominated administration with only a small Christian witness. They are a constant reminder to all of God's displeasure against those who choose to turn their back on the Almighty.

## What do the Messages Mean?

It is generally agreed that these messages can have three main applications.

### 1. The Seven Churches of John's day

The question that immediately comes to mind is, Why these seven churches? Why not Colosse, to which the apostle Paul wrote one of his epistles? Surely there were hundred's of churches spread throughout the world by this time - it was approximately 63 years after Pentecost!

The reason God choose these churches and not others can be simply put down to the fact that God is Sovereign, and will choose whom and what according to His Divine Will. They were literal churches with real problems, and were probably typical of the other churches of the day.

### 2. The Progressive State of God's Church

A study of history reveals that the church has gone through seven basic periods or stages. In a sense, the seven congregations could represent the consecutive and differing spiritual states of the church throughout the past 2000 years.

## 3. The Seven Characteristics existing Today

As the Book of Revelation portrays events from the point of view of the last days, those characteristics revealed by Christ in the 1st century church could all exist simultaneously among God's people as the world treks closer to the Second Advent.

In fact, we do not have to look too far to see among God's people those who;

\* Have left or forsaken their first love and zeal for Christ (Rev.2:4);

\* Are today suffering and persecuted for their faith in Christ (Rev.2:9);

\* Are strong in faith and remain true to the truth of the gospel (Rev. 2:13);

\* Seek to mislead fellow - Christians with false doctrines (Rev.2:20);

\* Are nominal members of the church but are spiritually dead (Rev.3:1);

\* Have kept the commandments, endured patiently, and persevered in God's ways (Rev.3:10);

\* Are spiritually proud, displaying great works with no spiritual value (Rev.3:17).

The commendation, condemnation, and counsel, given to each of the seven churches was finalized by a challenging benediction from our Lord: "*He who has an ear, let him hear what the Spirit says to the churches* " (Rev. 2:7,11,17,29; 3:6,13,22).

And the messages to the seven churches are messages that apply to all of God's people in whatever generation they might live. The most important lesson we can all learn from them is that true born-of-the-Spirit Christians must be concerned about each of the spiritual conditions we have just considered.

## Characteristics of the Seven Churches

In each of the letters to the seven churches, the common thread is Jesus speaking to members of His church. It is important to note that although the messages are directed to the church at a particular location, the contents are directed to the individual member of the church.

The letters respectively commend the churches for their strong spiritual works, and where appropriate they reprimand them about their specific problems and shortcomings.

One of the several attributes of Jesus' glory and majesty, as described in the first chapter, is repeated and placed at the heading of each letter to the seven churches. After the message finds its mark, a final word is given. God's people are encouraged not to close their hearts and minds to the solemn instructions of our Lord, but rather to listen to what the Spirit is saying to the churches.

The characteristics of the seven churches are summarized in the table as shown:

| Message / Church | Ephesus | Smyrna | Pergamum | Thyatira | Sardis | Philadelphia | Laodicea |
|---|---|---|---|---|---|---|---|
| COMMENDATION | • I know your deeds - your work of faith and labour of love • No compromise with false teaching • Loyalty in the church • Endurance | • I know your works • They were a persecuted church in an affluent society • Not rich in terms of material goods, but rich in spiritual matters | • Their works were known where Satan had his throne • Had not denied the faith even under persecution | • Their works of love, service, faith, patience were known • They were even working harder than before | • I know your works. You have a reputation of being alive - BUT | • An important witness in the area - • An open door • Not a strong church • They believed God's Word & kept it | • I know your works. • Not one word |
| CONDEMNATION | The people had left or forsaken their first love. | Not one word | • Some (but not all) hold to the doctrines of Balaam and the Nicolaitans • They ate food sacrificed to idols and committed sexual immorality | They bowed to the pressure of society and introduced the false doctrine of Jezebel | You are DEAD! | Not one word | • They were neither hot nor cold - rather they were luke - warm. • They were rich with material goods • They were wretched pitiful, poor, blind, and naked. |
| COUNSEL | Remember and Repent. | Do not be afraid of the suffering but be faithful unto death | Repent or else | Hold on to what you have until I come | • Wake -up • Strengthen the things that remain • Remember • Obey • Repent | Behold I come quickly. Let no man take your crown | • To buy refined gold • Buy white clothes • To put salve on the eyes • Be zealous & repent |
| CHALLENGE | Everyone who overcomes, qualifies to eat of the tree of life in the centre of God's garden. | To the overcomers - protection from the second death | The overcomers would be given "hidden Manna" and would receive a "white stone" | To the overcomers • Leadership and authority during the Millennium • The Morning Star | To the overcomers - • Dressed in white • Name will not be erased out of the "Book of Life" | To the overcomers - • A pillar in God's Temple • A passport to the New Jerusalem | To the overcomers is promised the right to enter the throne room in heaven |

The emphasis found in chapters 2 and 3 is on spiritual works. Words such a repentance, holiness, faithfulness, and the building of God-like characters, pervades the letters. A promise is made to each church and its members who overcome. That promise is an active part and direct involvement in the coming Kingdom of God - Eternal Life and rulership with Jesus over the nations.

The admonition to be zealous for God is urgent because the time of the Messiah's return is imminent. " *I am coming soon. Hold on to what you have, so that no-one will take your crown.*"

In these last days there is little doubt that we are living in a state of spiritual confusion. It is often difficult to tell who really is and who is not a Christian. Jesus reminded us that the "wheat" and "tares" would grow together in this age. We therefore need to be displaying the fruit of the Spirit so that we will be accounted blameless when we stand before the Judgment Seat of Christ. We need to be living day by day for the Lord as His servants and as His witnesses to a lost and degenerate society.

# Chapter 3

---

# Heaven Revealed

Up to this point in the book of Revelation we have not confronted any details about world conditions in the end-times. Chapters four and five of Revelation are a prelude to the book's real prophetic content.

In chapter four the central theme is the Throne of God in Heaven. It signifies God's absolute authority over all creation (Psalm 47:8).

In chapter five our attention is directed to the "Title Deed to Earth." The Lamb of God is seen holding a scroll sealed with seven seals (Rev.5:1). In Roman law, documents were sometimes sealed by seven witnesses. This emphasized that the contents of the documents were certain and true. In the Bible the number seven has the symbolic meaning of completeness.

## The Rapture of John

*"And after this I* (John) *looked and there before me was a door standing open in heaven. And a voice I had first heard speaking to me like a trumpet said, "Come up here ...."*

John wrote chapters one to three of Revelation from the island of Patmos as he was carried along

by the Spirit. In chapter four, however, John is
summoned to "*come up here* ." In other words,
John was caught up into heaven. This has given rise
to the suggestion that the church will be Raptured
before the Tribulation. However, if this were the
only reason or reference supporting the
Pretribulation Rapture of the church, the concept
would rest on very shaky grounds.

**Will the Church go through the Tribulation?**

There are several passages which give clear
reference to the fact that **the church will not go
through the Tribulation**

**1. The Promised Exemption from Trial**

Scripture clearly teaches that believers will be
kept from the "time of trial" (Rev. 3:10). This verse
is consistent with the Blessed Hope of Titus 2:13.

*"While we wait for the blessed hope - the glorious
appearing of our great God and Saviour, Jesus
Christ, who gave himself for us to redeem us from
all wickedness and to purify for himself a people
that are his very own, eager to do what is good."*

**2. Safety from the Wrath of God**

Many verses point to the fact that His Bride -
the church - will not suffer the Tribulation Wrath:
*"For God did not appoint us to suffer wrath but
to receive salvation through our Lord Jesus
Christ"* (1 Thess.5:9).

*"Since we have been justified by His blood, how much more shall we be saved from God's Wrath through Him!"* (Rom.5:9)
*"If this is so, then the Lord knows how to rescue godly men from trials and to hold the unrighteous for the day of judgment"* (2 Pet.2:9).

Other promises given to the church that assure us safety from the wrath of God:

**(a)** 1 Thess. 1:10   **(b)** Joel .2: 28-31
**(c)** Malachi 4:1   **(d)** Zeph.1: 14-18

## 3. The Promise of an Imminent Hope

*"Two men will be in the field; one will be taken and the other left. Two women will be grinding with a hand mill; one will be taken and the other left. Therefore keep watch, because you do not know on what day your Lord will come. But understand this: If the owner of the house had known at what time of the night the thief was coming, he would have kept watch and would not have let his house be broken into. So you also must be ready, because the Son of Man will come at an hour when you do not expect him"* (Matt. 24:40-44).

Other Biblical References

**(a)** John 14:3   **(b)** James 5:6
**(c)** Titus 2:12-13   **(d)** 1 John 2:28; 3:2-3

## 4. Revelation of the Man of Lawlessness

According to Daniel 9:27, the Antichrist will confirm a covenant with the nation of Israel for seven years. It should be noted that it is the signing of this "peace pact" that will commence the seven year Tribulation Period.

Now in the middle of the Tribulation - i.e., after three and one half years - he will stop or put an end to Jewish sacrifices in the rebuilt Temple located on Mount Moriah.

The Antichrist is the principal actor on Earth during the seven year Tribulation Period. Now the apostle Paul says in 2 Thess. 2:1-10 that the Antichrist ( or the lawless one) cannot be revealed until the **he** has been removed from the world.

" *For the secret power of lawlessness is already at work, but the one who now holds it back will continue to do so till* **HE** *is taken out of the way. And then the lawless one will be revealed, whom the Lord Jesus will overthrow with the breath of his mouth and destroy by the splendour of his coming.*"

## Who is the "He?"

Considerable confusion exists among many well respected Christian teachers and leaders relative to the ministry of the Holy Spirit during the Tribulation Period. Unfortunately much of this confusion has originated from the footnote in the Scofield Reference Bible on 2 Thessalonians 2:1-12. This footnote indicates that the Holy Spirit, the restraining influence on Satan the devil, will be removed when the church is Raptured just before the Tribulation begins.

In verse 7, the restrainer, or "*he that will be taken out of the way,*" is masculine and thus would refer to a person or individual who presently withholds or hinders the revelation of Antichrist.

## A number of possible interpretations

The most logical and plausible interpretations as to the identity of the restrainer are as follows:

### 1. The Holy Spirit

Since the work of the Holy Spirit is to convince ( John 8:46) and to convict (John 8: 9) men of sin, iniquity cannot reach its zenith until His removal. The restraining thing would then be the work of the Holy Spirit, which now acts as a Divine dam holding back the flood of iniquity such as the world has never seen before.

### 2. The Church

As the Holy Spirit abides and dwells within the believer, and the believer constitutes the church, therefore this body of believers in a sense exercises a restraining influence on the activities of Satan.

### 3. World Governments or Civil Powers

There are some scholars who believe that this restraining influence refers to three of the kings of the revived Roman Empire who will restrain the Antichrist during the first three-and-a-half years of the Tribulation ( Daniel 11). Quite apart from this school of thought, a number of today's governments do strive to maintain some measure of law, order, and righteousness. Some governments have considerable Christian influence within their administration and while this exists it is difficult to envisage the rise of the Antichrist.

## 4. The Determinate  Counsel of Almighty God
Those who hold to this view say that the Antichrist will not be revealed on this earth until a time predetermined in the mind and will of God.

## The  Most  Likely  Interpretation

The church is the temple  of  the  Holy  Spirit (1 Corinthians 3:16; Ephesians 2: 21-22) . When **she** is "caught up" or "Raptured", the Holy Spirit, **"He"**, will have lost His dwelling place here on this earth, and therefore will no longer have the vehicle ( men and women) to oppose the forces of evil.

In Genesis 6:3  God declared, " *My spirit will not always contend with [ or remain in] man.*" At that time the Holy Spirit abandoned a perverted society who were then swiftly judged by the flood.  But the Holy Spirit did not disappear.  He was still present then  and  He  will  be  for ever.  He is eternal ( Hebrews 9:14).

We  must  also  remember  that  the  Holy Spirit is omnipresent (Psalms.139: 7). Even after the departure of the church, which is His Temple, the Holy Spirit will still be working among mankind of good will.  Scripture reveals that during the Tribulation Period **"He"**, **the Holy Spirit**, will be poured out on Israel resulting in her conversion to their Messiah (Isaiah 59: 20-21;  Ezekiel 39: 29; Zechariah 12:10).  Now  we know that during the same period, that is, the period of the Great Tribulation a large multitude that no-one could count, from every nation, tribe, people, and language, will be redeemed from the earth. These people must be the Gentiles (Revelation 7:9,14).

Now it is impossible to believe in Christ without the aid of the Holy Spirit (1 Corinthians 12:3). It will, therefore, be necessary for Him to continue at least a part of His ministry on earth during this time of judgment.

## The Redeemed Multitude

Verse 9 of Revelation chapter 7 then paints a small picture of a vast crowd of people who will be saved during the Tribulation Period. If they are not redeemed from earth during this period, then where do they come from? If, on the other hand, they are redeemed from earth, but the Holy Spirit was absent, how then was it possible to obtain salvation?

The answer is quite simple. This mighty revival is a result of the power of God's Holy Spirit working through dedicated vessels - the 144,000 sealed Israelites already scattered around the world. The people from "*all nations, tribes, and languages*" indicate the extent and magnitude of this revival, and is rivalled only by the first-century moving of the Spirit of God, when "*the gospel was proclaimed to every creature under heaven*" (Colossians 1:23). However there is one vital difference in this revival from that of the first century. During this Tribulation Period every tribe will not only hear the gospel but will also have many of its members respond to salvation just prior to the return to this earth of Jesus Christ

We indeed should continually praise God for His unfailing love and mercy!

**In conclusion:** if the Rapture can take place only at the mid-point or the end of the Tribulation, then there is no basis for saying that Jesus can come at any time. We would therefore know when Christ is coming, and this is contrary to Scripture (Matt.24:36).   Importantly, if we can see Christ only after the Tribulation, it would be better to die before the Tribulation!

## The Throne of God

The central object of heaven is the throne of God. What John sees immediately he is Raptured in the Spirit is nothing short of the seat of government of the entire universe. This scene can be compared to another in the book of Revelation. Man's present governmental system, with its many corrupt practices, is to be shut down and destroyed (Rev.18). Today's world, led and inspired by the Devil, will be replaced by the Messiah's righteous and just Kingdom. Like a thread, this theme runs consistently through the book.

There are <u>seven</u> (7) distinct characteristics of the Throne of God:
**1. The Lamb is on the Throne.**
We know that God the Father is on the throne

We also know that God the Father cannot be seen (Jn.1:18; 6:46). The one whom John saw, sitting upon the throne, was none other than the only member of the Trinity who can be seen - the Lord Jesus Christ.

He is described as having the appearence of jasper and carnelian, and a rainbow, resembling an emerald encircled the throne. Being confronted with such a description of our Lord, we are entitled to ask two questions:

**a)** Did such a description have significance to the early Christian church?

**b)** Does it have any meaning for Christian today?

The jasper of Revelation is not the reddish/ opaque semi-precious stone we know today. Revelation 21:11 suggests that the jasper of Biblical times was a clear precious gem, and is more likely to be a diamond, the most brilliant of all precious stones.

Carnelian is a semi-precious stone which in colour is blood red.   In ancient times it was considered to be a precious gem, and more than likely resembled today's ruby.

Thus the two stones together remind us today of **glory**(white & radiant) and **sacrifice** (blood red). Both stones are incorporated in the walls of the New Jerusalem - God's Holy City that comes down from above and dwells with mankind on the New Earth in the Eternal State (Rev. 21:19,20).

The Hebrew people of the early Christian church would instantly recall that these two stones were the first and last stones in the breastplate of the High Priest (Ex. 28:17-20). Those stones also bore the names of the tribes of Israel, arranged according to the order of birth of the twelve patriarchs.

The first born son of Jacob, later renamed by God as Israel, was Reuben whose name means "behold a son." The last born to Israel was Benjamin, meaning "son of my right hand." Thus to the Hebrew Christians the two stones would suggest that Jesus Christ our great High Priest was enthroned at the father's side and reigning in power.

We also notice a rainbow, resembling an emerald encircling the throne. This is no ordinary rainbow. Today we see only half a rainbow in the sky. That is, we have only imperfect salvation while on this earth. When we reach heaven our salvation is complete, just as the rainbow is complete and whole, resembling the colour of an emerald. This precious stone speaks of Christ as the Eternal One.

## 2. The Twenty- Four Elders.

*"Surrounding the throne were twenty-four other thrones and seated on them were twenty-four elders."*

There has been considerable debate and controversy as to the identity of these 24 distinguished elders. Many very well-respected Bible scholars believe them to be men, some suggesting them to be the twelve leaders of the tribes of Israel which represent the Old Testament people, and the twelve apostles representing the

New Testament people.

There is another school of thought consisting of equally competent people who believe them to be angels.

It is not my desire to present in detail both sides of the debate but rather to point out that Scripture does not really make it abundantly clear as to whether they are men or angels. It is sufficient to say that whether men or angels or both, they are God's inner cabinet and worship leaders of the heavenly universe.

## 3. The Signs of Judgment.

*"From the throne came flashes of lightning, rumblings, and peals of thunder."*

Lightning and thunder have long been associated with the concept of judgment. What we then have in this chapter is a prelude to the judgment that is about to fall on mankind on planet earth. We will consider in detail these judgments which are described in chapters 6 through 19.

## 4. The Seven Spirits of God.

*"Before the throne, seven lamps were blazing. These are the seven spirits of God."*

The fact of there being seven spirits does not mean there are seven Holy Spirits, but this rather refers to the seven-fold working or characteristics of the Holy Spirit, as revealed in Isaiah 11:2:

1. the Spirit of the Lord;
2. the Spirit of Wisdom;
3. the Spirit of Understanding;
4. the Spirit of Counsel;
5. the Spirit of Power;
6. the Spirit of Knowledge;
7. the Spirit of the Fear of the Lord.

## 5. The Sea of Glass.

"*Also before the throne there was what looked like a sea of glass, clear as crystal.*"

This is an interesting expression. In Scripture, a sea usually refers to people. This idea is consistent with the scene in Revelation chapter 15. Here we see the Tribulation Saints who have been martyred by the forces of the Antichrist standing on what looked like a sea of glass.

It would seem that the expression "sea of glass" in this chapter refers to the great church victorious- the church at rest in Heaven from the turmoil and strife of this world.

## 6. The Four Living Creatures.

"*In the centre, around the throne, were four living creatures, and they were covered with eyes in front and behind.*"

As we study the description of these creatures, we find they take on animal-like characteristics - a lion, a ox or calf, a man, and a flying eagle.

These four living creatures are seraphim - a special class or order of angels. The seraphim are closely associated with the glory of God and in this incident they are engaged constantly in the worship of God, but their form would suggest they have other duties to perform.

Isaiah 6:3 presents the seraphim hovering above and on both sides of Jehovah on the throne. It is obvious from this description that they perform a priestly type of service for God. Succinctly put, their purpose is to show forth Jehovah's Holiness.

The very name seraphim, which means "burning ones," speaks of their consuming devotion to God.

## 7. The Heavenly Worship of Christ.

*"Each of the four living creatures......... never stop saying: Holy, Holy, Holy is the Lord God Almighty, who was, and is, and is to come. Whenever the living creatures give glory, honour and thanks to him who sits on the throne....... the twenty-four elders fall down before him...... and worship him."*

This describes the fact that the Lord Jesus Christ is the object of worship in heaven, and just as John stood before the throne to witness this marvellous sight, so we as the bridegroom's bride will one day, in the not too distant future, stand in awe and worship the Lord God Almighty.

## The Title-Deed to Earth

Chapter five directs the reader's attention to a scroll in the right hand of the one who sat upon the throne. This scroll had writing on both sides and was sealed with seven seals.

There can be little doubt as to the importance of this scroll, as determined by the events which follow. It was a very confidential document. No one knew the contents of this book except God. There seemed to be a **problem** which caused John to weep: "*I wept and wept because no-one was found who was worthy to open the scroll or look inside.*"

But then there was really no problem at all because the **person** in the form of: "...... *the Lion of the tribe of Judah......... the Lamb that had been slain,*" was able to take the scroll and open it. This person of course is none other than the omnipotent and Eternal Christ.

It is interesting to note that the elder, who belongs to one of the special order of angels, saw the Christ as a Lion, whereas John saw Jesus Christ as a Lamb!

The explanation for this is really very simple. John was the beloved disciple of Jesus. In fact, John was the only disciple who stayed with his Master through the crucifixion. John sees Jesus as the sacrificial Lamb, for he sees Him through eyes of faith. The elder, who had never experienced the redemption process, would not view Christ as a Lamb but rather a Lion, indicating strength and might.

Men who reject Christ will one day see Him as a Lion when He comes to judge and reign over them. Men who are believers will see Him as their sacrificial Lamb.

The Problem was solved by the Person of Jesus Christ. What followed was the **Practice** that all Christians should do daily - **Worship.** The elders bowed down and worshipped Christ. "*They sang a new song, you are worthy............*" In ourselves we are not worthy to see God, but through His death Christ made us worthy. God has made us His sons and daughters, and it is because we belong to Him that we shall reign with Him throughout Eternity.

The final section of chapter five is devoted to **Praise**, with a countless number of angels praising God. The living Bible says there were "millions." The NIV Bible suggests even "billions."

Worthy is the Lamb that was slain to receive:

1. Power;
2. Riches;
3. Wisdom;
4. Strength;
5. Honour;
6. Glory;
7. Praise.

We note the Word of God says that all creatures worshipped the Lamb. Praise and worship is not an optional extra in the Christian's diary. It is an requirement to be practised daily. Worship is a life-style, and not something we do on Sunday.

All Christians should read Psalm 100 often, and practise the words of the Psalmist in their daily lives. At times we do not always understand God's Word or Will for our lives. But during these last days we must trust Him, for He knows what is best for us.

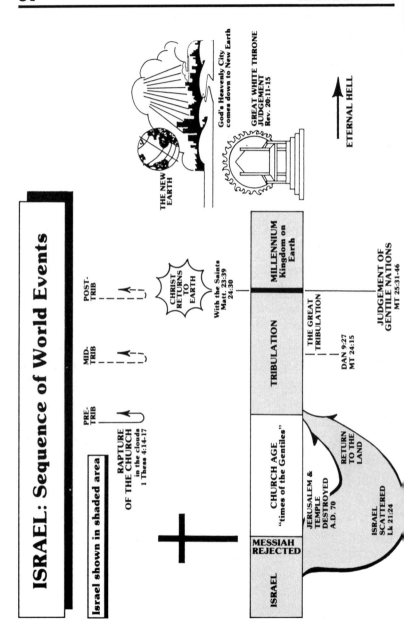

ISRAEL: Sequence of World Events

Israel shown in shaded area

PRE-TRIB — RAPTURE OF THE CHURCH in the clouds 1 Thess 4:14-17

MID-TRIB

POST-TRIB

CHRIST RETURNS TO EARTH — With the Saints Matt. 23:39 24:30

THE NEW EARTH

God's Heavenly City comes down to New Earth

GREAT WHITE THRONE JUDGEMENT Rev. 20:11-15

ETERNAL HELL

ISRAEL

MESSIAH REJECTED

CHURCH AGE "times of the Gentiles"

JERUSALEM & TEMPLE DESTROYED A.D. 70

RETURN TO THE LAND

ISRAEL SCATTERED Lk 21:24

TRIBULATION

THE GREAT TRIBULATION DAN 9:27 MT 24:15

MILLENNIUM Kingdom on Earth

JUDGEMENT OF GENTILE NATIONS MT 25:31-46

# Chapter 4

---

# Gathering Clouds
# Cast their Shadows-
# The Tribulation Period

As we come to the sixth chapter of the book of Revelation we are immediately confronted with the darkest period of this world's history. Nothing in the past compares with the events that will follow during the next seven years.

However, to fully comprehend what the Tribulation Period as described in the book of Revelation is all about, one must understand that it is a very special time in the plan of God for His **nation Israel.** To see this more clearly, we must turn to the book of Daniel and examine briefly the prophecy of Daniel's seventy weeks of years.

### The Time of Jacob's Trouble

Daniel was one of the young Hebrew teenagers taken captive to Babylon by king Nebuchadnezzar in 606 B.C. Ezekiel was captured during the second raid by Nebuchadnezzar in 598 B.C. Jeremiah was the prophet who remained behind in Jerusalem to minister to the remnant of Jews after the city was destroyed in 586 B.C.

Jeremiah the prophet wrote in chapter 30:3-7 these words:

> *"The days are coming declares the Lord, when I will bring my people Israel and Judah back from captivity and restore them to the land I gave to their forefathers to possess, says the Lord."*

What then follows is the Divine description of the Jews in the time of the Tribulation- or, as often referred to, " the Great Tribulation."

> *"This is what the Lord says: cries of fear are heard- terror, not peace. Ask and see. Can a man bear children? Then why do I see every strong man with his hands on his stomach like a woman in labour, every face turned deathly pale? How awful that day will be! None will be like it. It will be a time of trouble for Jacob (* time of Jacob's trouble), *but he will be saved out of it."*

Now all that Jeremiah has said is the same as God told Daniel concerning the time of trouble for the nation, and as the Lord told His disciples about the Great Tribulation (Matt.25; Lk.21).

Why did Jeremiah call it the "time of Jacob's trouble"?  Simply because it is a judgment of God upon the Jewish nation as a result of their rejection of the Messiah. It is not a judgment for the church. The church will not be on earth when the Tribulation judgments fall specifically on Israel, but also generally on the rest of the  world for their attitude against God's chosen people and their rejection of the Saviour of the world.

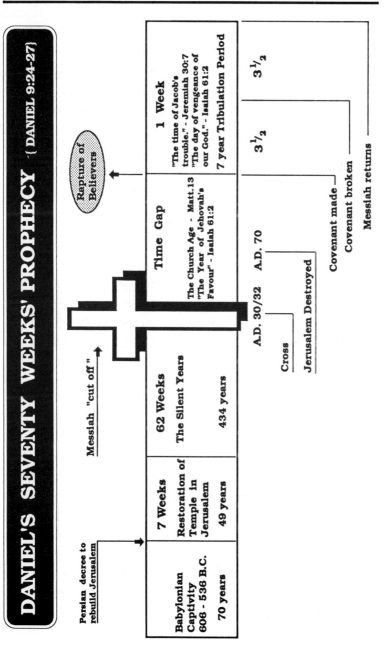

DANIEL'S SEVENTY WEEKS' PROPHECY [DANIEL 9:24-27]

Persian decree to rebuild Jerusalem

Messiah "cut off"

Rapture of Believers

| Babylonian Captivity 606 - 536 B.C. | 7 Weeks Restoration of Temple in Jerusalem | 62 Weeks The Silent Years | Time Gap The Church Age - Matt.13 "The Year of Jehovah's Favour" - Isaiah 61:2 | 1 Week "The time of Jacob's trouble." - Jeremiah 30:7 "The day of vengeance of our God." - Isaiah 61:2 7 year Tribulation Period |
|---|---|---|---|---|
| 70 years | 49 years | 434 years | | $3\frac{1}{2}$          $3\frac{1}{2}$ |

A.D. 30/32   A.D. 70

Cross

Jerusalem Destroyed

Covenant made

Covenant broken

Messiah returns

# The Seventy Weeks' Prophecy

Daniel was a godly man living in a pagan land, having been taken captive from Jerusalem to Babylon by king Nebuchadnezzar. He desired God to grant him understanding regarding the future of his people, the Jews. He was subsequently told,

> "*Seventy sevens are decreed for your people and the holy city to finish transgression, to put an end to sin, to atone for wickedness, to bring in everlasting righteousness, to seal up vision and prophecy and to anoint the most holy*" (Dan.9:24).

Now it is important to understand the time elements involved, and reference to the chart on page 37 should clarify any misunderstanding.

The Hebrew word translated "week" actually means a unit of seven rather than a specific number of days. In this case, a week refers to a period of 7 years. It is the context of the passage which reveals the length of time involved. The word should literally be translated "sevens" or "heptads."

The seventy sevens meant that there would be a period of 490 years from the decree issued by King Cyrus to rebuild Jerusalem before the Jews would be restored to Divine favour when the Messiah would come and reign from the Holy City.

The word translated "decreed" or "determined" means more than an expression of will. It could be correctly rendered "divided," and the context shows that the 490 years were actually to be divided up into three (3) sections:

**1.** First division- seven sevens or 49 years.
**2.** Second division- sixty-two sevens or 434 years.
**3.** Third division - one seven or 7 years

At the end of the second division, the Messiah would be "cut-off" or crucified (Dan.9:26). At the same time the Romans would destroy the Holy city and the Temple and would scatter the Jews among the nations as was foretold 1000 years earlier by Moses, that great giver of the Law to the Hebrew people (Deut.28:49-68).

Now the message that God showed Daniel was this: At the very time the Jews would reject their Messiah, they themselves would come to be rejected. God's time clock would stop for them. There was never any plan for them to be permanently rejected, but only to be put on hold, as Romans chapter 11:25-27 clearly indicates. This is consistent with the essentials of the covenants made by God with Abraham, Isaac, Jacob and David (Gen.12; 13; 15; 17; 18; 22; 26; 28).

So we see there has been a very long break, certainly in man's timing, before God's clock recommences. Almost 2000 years have passed called the "Church Age," but the time is fast approaching when the hands will reach midnight, and the final seven years of the prophecy will be played out in a small and desolate country called Israel.

## When will God's Clock begin Ticking?

During the whole of the interval period except for the past 44 years ( since 1948), the Jews have been scattered throughout the world. But we have seen in these last four years, under the leadership of the modern day King Cyrus, President of the Soviet Union, Mikhail Gorbachev, literally hundred of thousands of Jews from around the world, particularly from Russia, returning to their homeland to wait the coming of the Messiah.

It is during this same interval of time that Christ is gathering for Himself a people from among the Gentile Nations, a people called the church or the Body of Christ.

It is when the church is complete, or as the apostle Paul says in Romans 11:25: "*.... the full number of the Gentiles has come in,*" and has been called up into Heaven, that the final week of years regarding the Jews is to resume. It is then the Temple will be rebuilt on Mount Moriah and the Jews will again recommence Temple sacrifices in unbelief. However, their joy will be short-lived. At the mid-way point of the Tribulation, the Jews will be confronted with the forces of the Antichrist who will set up an image in the Temple and cause the "*abomination of desolation*", as recorded by Daniel and referred to by Jesus in the Olivet discourse in Matthew 24:15.

This will be "*the time of Jacob's trouble.*" - a time when the hardened hearts of the Jewish people will smelt under the weight of God's Divine judgments. But those who have received and kept the word of Divine patience will then be spared from the hour of trial that is to come upon the whole world, to test those who live on the earth (Rev.3:10).

# Chapter 5

---

# The Seal Judgments

The first of the three chronological judgments representing periods of the Tribulation, the seals, trumpets, and bowls, are briefly described in chapter 6. They are part of the script written on both sides of the scroll (Rev.5:1).

This scroll referred to in Revelation was not the same kind of book we use today. It was one long sheet of parchment, rolled into a scroll. Words were written on both sides. This particular scroll had seven seals that had to be opened.

Jesus the Lamb is seen unrolling the scroll and opening each of the seals. John is an eye-witness to the pageant. In fact, he is invited into the front row to record the contents of the activity graphically depicted in his presence: "I watched.......I heard....... I looked."

What did John observe?

### The Four Horsemen of the Apocalypse

### 1. The First Seal: vv.1-2

With the breaking of the first of the seven seals we see a picture of a **White Horse.** This white horse is mounted by a rider who "*held a bow, and was given a crown, and he rode forth to conquer.*" The fact that the rider had a bow but no arrows suggests that he will endeavour to restore order and peace to a world that is in turmoil.

In Revelation chapter 19 Jesus Christ is seen riding a white horse as He comes with His saints to set up His Kingdom and reign for a thousand years on this earth. In this chapter we see a picture of a false Messiah, an antichrist who will seek to bring about a false peace on the earth by deception.

## Why will the World be in Turmoil?

According to the apostle Paul's letter to the Thessalonian Christians, the Antichrist or the lawless one cannot commence his evil activities in the world until the church has been Raptured. The Rapture or removal of millions of born-again Christians will create havoc in every facet of political and economic life throughout the world.

Furthermore, according to Ezekiel's prophecy, Russia and its allies will be destroyed on the northern hills of Israel by God (Ezek.38-39). However, the world will attribute victory to the Nation of Israel. Such a decisive annihilation of the vast army from the north will send shock-waves around the globe. The newly formed United States of Europe will see an immediate threat from Israel. As a result of this turmoil in the Middle East, the powerful figurehead of the Antichrist will emerge to bring calm in an otherwise feverish boiling cauldron of anxiety.

## 2. The Second Seal: vv.3-4
When the Lamb opens the second seal, a fiery red horse goes forth to take peace from the earth.

This **Red Horse** is obviously a symbol of war and blood-shed, for he has the ability to "*take peace from the earth, and to make men slay each other.*"

Satan has always destroyed life. Now he works through the Antichrist to destroy mankind.

## 3. The Third Seal: vv.5-6

When the next seal is broken, John sees a rider on a **Black Horse** with a pair of scales in his hand. A voice accompanies the vision. It announces, "*A quart of wheat for a day's wages, and three quarts of barley for a day's wages, and do not damage the oil and the wine.*"

A number of translations have the word "denarius" instead of "day's wages." The denarius was a Roman silver coin and was equal in value to the daily wage of a working man (Matt.20:2).

What this prophecy is saying is that world-wide famine as a result of war will in turn result in worldwide inflation. It will know no bounds. The living Bible says that a loaf of bread will cost about $20Aust. Certainly what we are presently experiencing is a foreshadow of the closeness of the coming day of judgment.

It is also interesting to note that in the midst of such poverty, the rich are sheltered from the scarcity of goods and services. The rider on the black horse was instructed not to "*hurt the oil and the wine,*" which are the traditional foods of the rich. As is the case with all wars and resulting famine, this famine will take a heavy toll on the common people.

## 4. The Fourth Seal: vv.7-8

The opening of the fourth seal introduces us to a **Pale Horse.** As the seal is opened Satan uses two things he has always used against God's people:

**a) Death.** The pale horse ( or corpse-like horse) is symbolic of death. He destroys love, liberty, and life.

**b) Destruction.** Since the time God created man, Satan has been busy destroying God's people and the things of God.

A fourth of the world's population will die by the sword, famine, and plague during the time of the judgments.

**Note:** It is important to understand that the four horsemen judgments are not four single events that occur in a chronological sequence. Rather, they are simultaneous judgments occurring throughout and at different times during the seven year period. The horsemen are symbolic of conditions and events that will occur on earth over the seven years of Tribulation.

Jesus also spoke of the conditions represented by the four horsemen(see Matt.24; Mk.13; Lk.21).

## 5. The Fifth Seal: vv. 9-11

The opening of the fifth seal pictures a time of Great Tribulation. The vision that John saw was the souls under the altar of those who:

**a)** Preached the gospel during the first half of the Tribulation and were killed for their witness.

**b)** Lived and obeyed the Word of God, and testified of His saving grace.

**c)** Refused to follow the Antichrist and worship

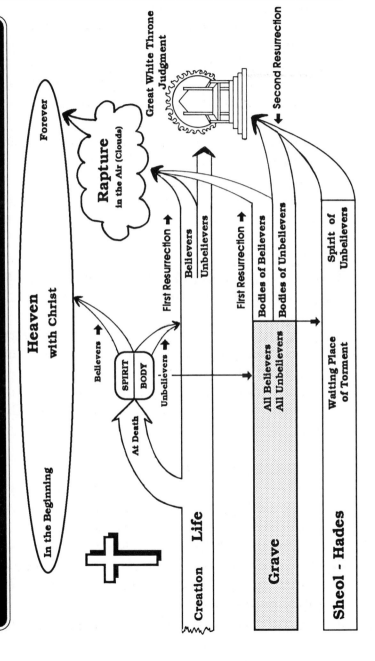

The Period for Mankind between DEATH and RESURRECTION

the material wealth of this world.

These martyrs ask an important question, a question that Christians sometimes ask today. They want to know how long it will be before their murderers are bought to justice, and for God to bring judgment upon the whole world?

God sometimes chooses to delay His judgment for reasons best known to a Sovereign and righteous judge. This does not mean He will forego it.

The answer the martyred saints were given was simply a word of encouragement to be patient, since others would be martyred for the sake of the gospel.

## What Group of People will live on Earth at some time during the Tribulation?

**a)** No truly born again Christians. They will have been Raptured prior to the commencement of the Tribulation Judgments.

**b)** Carnal Christians who have never made a confession of their guilt and belief in Jesus Christ.

**c)** All non-believers.

## 6. The Sixth Seal: vv.12-17

When the sixth seal is opened, the earth is violently shaken by a giant earthquake, indicating that it is the "Great Day of God's wrath." Following the persecution of the saints, God will show His displeasure by shaking the Earth. " *There was a great earthquake. The sun turned black like sackcloth made of goats' hair,the whole moon turned blood red, and the stars of the sky fell to earth.  The sky* receded like a scroll, rolling up, and every mountain and island was removed from its place."

When we compare this description of the sixth seal with what Jesus said would happen at the end of the Tribulation, we gauge something of the holocaust that will engulf the earth throughout those seven years. "*Immediately after the distress of those days, the sun will be darkened, and the moon will not give  its light; the stars will fall from the sky. and the heavenly bodies will be shaken*" (Matt.24:29).

The sixth chapter of Revelation, then, commences the literal judgments of the Tribulation Period. In  this chapter we  have  six basic conditions outlined:

**(1)** The rise of the counterfeit Christ;
**(2)** Escalation and intensity of wars;
**(3)** Worldwide famines;
**(4)** Disease epidemics;
**(5)** Great persecution and tribulation;
**(6)** Cosmic disturbances.

The last verse of the chapter reveals what follows the heavenly signs, "*For the great day of their (the Triune God)  wrath has come, and who can stand?* "

### The Wrath of God

This wrath of God is a basic theme in Revelation. The day of the Lord is a day of wrath and retribution (Isa.2:10-21;13:6-16; Zeph.1:14-18).   This is not a case of  God being spiteful, but rather God's response to a stubbon and unrepentant world.

The prophet Joel put the day of God's wrath into chronological perspective. He wrote, "*And afterwards I will pour out my spirit on all people.....I will pour out my Spirit in those days. I will show wonders in the heavens and on the earth, blood and fire and billows of smoke. The sun will be turned to darkness and the moon to blood before the coming of the great and dreadful day of the Lord.*"

The key to understanding this passage is the words-"*And afterwards......in those days*" What does this refer to? The passage has an obvious reference to the days of the Tribulation Period. The Holy Spirit will not indwell people as He does today, but will occupy a ministry similar to that during the Old Testament days. Under the influence of the 144,000 Jewish witnesses, a great multitude of people will be saved during the Tribulation Period.

As a result of these horrific seal judgments we have an account of the greatest prayer meeting in history. But they prayed for the wrong thing. The only way to protect the sinner from the wrath of the Lamb is the righteousness of the Lamb.

The great displays in the Heavens and on the Earth will all occur before the coming of the great day of the Lord God Almighty. This will be the day Jesus Christ will return to Earth with His saints: "*He will come with clouds, and every eye will see Him, even those who pierced Him; and all the people of the Earth will mourn because of Him. So shall it be! Amen.*" (Rev. 1:7).

# Chapter 6

---

# The Great Soul Harvest of the Tribulation

The opening of the first six seals results in calamitous events breaking out all over the world, but to some degree there will be a concentration of destruction around the Middle East region. This is where the main forces of the Antichrist will be located.

Chapter seven brings a breath of fresh air into the commentary. The location shifts from Earth to Heaven. The chapter picks up the story of God's people and answers the question of Revelation 6:17: "*For the great day of God's wrath has come, and who can stand?*"

John now sees the security of the faithful who have come out of the Great Tribulation, and this presents a marked contrast to a sinful world facing almost total destruction.

## The Sealed Servants of God

John observes four angels standing at the four corners of the earth, holding back the four winds so that they will not blow on the earth. **Why?** These winds represent the universal judgment and retribution that is to come upon the whole earth (cf. Dan 7:2; Matt. 24:31; Rev.14:18;16:5). The angels are holding back these judgments so John can see who it is that can stand during this time.

Immediately after the four winds' vision, John hears another angel say, "*Do not harm the land or the sea or the trees until we put a seal on the foreheads of the servants of our God*" (Rev.7:3). This seal will put an everlasting mark of "*His father's name written on their foreheads*" (Rev 14:1).

We are not told of what this seal will consist, but the text suggests it will be visible.

### What is the Significance of the Sealing?

In ancient times seals were used for different purposes as is the case today. A seal is used in official legal documents to signify the authenticity of a transaction. One seals a letter in an envelope for privacy. A seal can also be used as a means of identification or ownership.

The sealing by God of these 144,000 people was absolutely necessary for two reasons:

**1.** For identification, showing ownership to God. In a symbolic way the seal is saying that these people belong to God.

**2.** They are sealed for protection from the afflictions and persecutions by the Antichrist. With destruction and judgment falling all around them, it would be easy for these evangelists to be killed before their specific task of taking the gospel to every part of the globe is completed (refer Matt.24:14).

It is interesting to note that during the same period of time, mankind will be forced to take another mark on their right hand or on their forehead (Rev.13: 14-18). This mark is known as the "mark of the beast."

We know that 144,000 Jewish witnesses will be sealed and marked by God. It may well be that believers will have the mark of God on their foreheads, whereas all unbelievers alive during the Tribulation Period will feature the mark of the Antichrist. This mark will be final and will say to the world that those so marked are enemies of God.

## Who are the 144,000 servants of God?

The Bible is quite specific about this group of people.

**1.**They belong to God. They are His servants.

**2.** They have a visible mark on their foreheads. This will assist with identification by God's angels when judgment is falling all around them.

**3.**They are located on this earth during the Tribulation Period. They will experience but be protected from the judgments of God.

**4.** They are a specific number of persons.There is no reason not to take the number as literally 144,000 - not one more or one less.

**5.** They are Jews. There are no Gentiles in this company

**6.** They are all from one of the twelve tribes of Israel. We note that the tribe of Levi is substituted for the tribe of Dan, and the tribe of Joseph is substituted for the tribe of Ephraim. This is probably

a judgment of God against them for their desire to
be involved with wickedness and idolatry (cf. Gen.
49:17; Num.13; Deut.29:18-21; 1 Kings 12:25-30).

### Who are the Multitude in White Robes?

Verse 9 paints a picture of a vast multitude of
people who will be saved during the Tribulation
Period, a crowd so vast that it is described as "*a
great multitude that no-one could count.*" It is an
innumerable company of people from all nations
surrounding the throne. They are clothed in white
which represents the righteousness of Christ. The
palms in their hands represent victory.

This group of people are vastly different from
the 144,000. They are predominantly Gentiles
because they come from every nation, tribe, people,
and language. Their vast number would indicate
the extent of the revival and the effectiveness of the
preaching of the sealed Jews.

They praise God for their salvation which was
provided by the Lamb. They took pleasure in
thanking and praising God. Should we not always
show appreciation for the price of our salvation?

In verse 12 they sing a great benediction.
"*Amen! Praise and glory and wisdom and thanks
and honour and power and strength to be our God
for ever and ever, Amen!*"

**Who are these people?**   They are the ones
saved out of the first three and one half years of the
Tribulation Judgments. Their robes were washed in
the blood of the Lamb, and they serve God daily
before the throne in Heaven.

These Tribulation saints constitute a distinctive category along with the church, the Old Testament saints, the 144,000, the two super witnesses of Revelation chapter 11, and the martyred saints of the last half of the Tribulation. These particular saints will be raised at the Second Coming of Jesus Christ (Rev.14:13; 20:4).

Each group of people have their own relationship to Christ, depending upon the period of time in which these individuals were converted. Each group in various special ways will serve the risen Christ for all eternity.

A very valuable lesson and principle can be applied from this chapter in Revelation, and it is this. One should not say, "I'll wait until the Tribulation to accept Christ. After all, if Christ comes and takes the Church and I am left behind, I will get a 'second chance'."

This is not so, because no one knows if he or she will live that long. No one knows if he might die in his sleep before the Rapture of the church. On the other hand if a person cannot accept Christ with the true church present on earth, and with the Holy Spirit active in the lives of all true believers, how much harder will it be to come to Christ during this most difficult time?

Christ's coming may be near or it could be years from now. In the meantime, death may come, giving a person no second chance for salvation. "..... *Now is the time of God's favour, now is the day of salvation*" (2 Cor. 6:2).

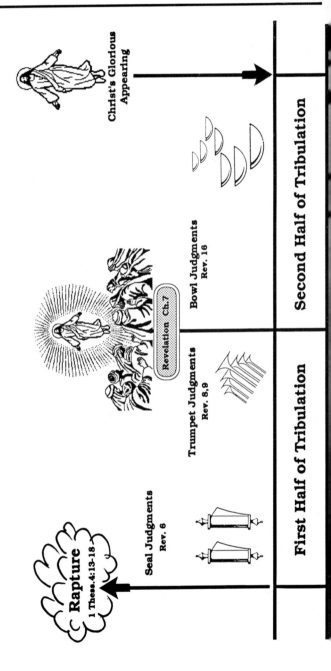

The Great Soul Harvest of the Tribulation

Rapture
1 Thess. 4:13-18

Seal Judgments
Rev. 6

Trumpet Judgments
Rev. 8,9

Revelation Ch.7

Bowl Judgments
Rev. 16

Christ's Glorious Appearing

First Half of Tribulation

Second Half of Tribulation

# Chapter 7

---

# The Four Trumpet Plagues of the Seventh Seal

We now come to the eighth chapter of Revelation and the opening of the seventh and final seal. Here we have a conclusive example that the seal, trumpet and bowl judgments are sequential. It is the opening of the seventh seal that commences the trumpet judgments.

*"And when he had opened the seventh seal, there was silence in Heaven for about half an hour."* This marks the only occasion in recorded history that heaven is silent. There is not the slightest sound or movement, and we ask, **Why?**

There are three (3) possible explanations:

**The Purpose for the Silence:**

**1.** The judgments to fall on the world are so shocking that a time of silence must be taken to consider what is to come. It is a dramatic pause or lull before the final storm of God's wrath.

**2.** During the sixth seal, mankind seemed to weaken for the first time during the Tribulation. A merciful and patient God now pauses and awaits further repentance. God takes no pleasure in the death of the wicked (Ezek.33:11).

## The Duration of the Silence:

**3.** We are told that it lasted for 30 minutes. The number thirty in the Bible is often associated with mourning. Israel mourned for thirty days over the death of Aaron (Num.20:29) and Moses(Deut. 34:8).

> *"Another angel, who had a golden censer, came and stood at the altar. He was given much incense to offer, with the prayers of the saints on the golden altar before the throne"* (8:3).

In chapter 5:8 we note that the four living creatures and the twenty-four elders held golden bowls full of incense, which were the prayers of the saints.

It would seem from both these references that the unanswered prayers of God's people may be stored by these administrative angels until the time for their answer, at which time they are used in the worship of heaven. A part of the Lord's prayer is a typical example of as yet unanswered prayer.

The trumpet plagues are poised to strike. It is interesting to note the role that trumpets have played in the Hebrew culture. They were used to assemble the people together, to move the tribes, and to celebrate the festivals. They were also used to sound the alarm in time of war and in the coronation of kings.

The Old Testament prophet Zephaniah wrote of this time when the trumpets would herald the day of God's wrath:

> *"The great day of the Lord is near and coming quickly. Listen! The cry on the day*

*of the Lord will be bitter........ That day will be a day of wrath, a day of distress and anguish, a day of trouble and ruin.... of darkness and gloom....of clouds and blackness,* **a day of trumpet and battle cry** *against the fortified cities and against the corner towers"* (Zeph.1:15,16)

These punishments are intended to lead the human race to repentance. Tragically, for the most part humanity refuses to heed the warnings and yield to the hostilities directed against the Creator of the universe (Rev.9:20).

The first four trumpet plagues strike the earth itself, creating an ecological catastrophe of global proportions. The visions present spectacular light and sound shows:

## 1. The First Trumpet: v.7

The sound of the first trumpet announces God's curse upon nature. Hail and fire mixed with blood was cast upon the earth. One-third of the trees and all green grass was burned up.

It has been observed that plant life was the first living matter to be created, and it is now the first to be destroyed (Gen.1:11,12).

## 2. The Second Trumpet: vv.8-9

John now sees *"something like a huge mountain all ablaze, thrown into the sea."* One third of all ocean life dies and a third of all the ships are destroyed.

This great mountain burning with fire may refer to a meteoritic mass as it enters the earth's atmosphere and falls out of the sky into the sea, possibility the Mediterranean Sea.

### 3. The Third Trumpet: vv.10-11

The third angel's trumpet sounds and John sees "*a great star, blazing like a torch fall from the sky on a third of the rivers and on the springs of water.*" This star destroys one third of the world's water supply.

The star could refer to a meteorite containing poisonous and bitter gases which falls on the alpine regions of the world and all other fresh water sources. We note that during the second trumpet judgments a third of the salt waters were contaminated. Now a third of the earth's fresh water supplies suffer a similar fate.

The star or meteorite was named "Wormwood." Wormwood is a perennial bitter herb which grows naturally throughout Palestine. All species of the Wormwood herb have a strong, bitter taste.

### 4. The Fourth Trumpet: v.12

As the fourth trumpet sounded, great disturbances in the atmosphere occurred. "*A third of the sun was struck, a third of the moon, a third of the stars, so that a third of them turned dark.*"

This judgment will result in a dimming of daylight and a deepening of the nighttime. The world will have to contend with only eight hours of daylight and sixteen hours of darkness.

The Old Testament prophecy of Amos foreshadows such a day: "*In that day, declares the Sovereign Lord, I will make the sun go down at noon and darken the earth in broad daylight*" (Amos 8:9).

It was on the fourth day that God created the heavenly bodies - sun, moon, and stars (Gen.1:14-16). They were to be for "*signs, and for seasons, and for days, and for years.*"  After the flood God promised not to alter this divine arrangement (Gen.8:22). But in the Tribulation, during the fourth trumpet judgments, earth's light will be limited by those judgments.

### Three Trumpet Judgments to come!

The final three angelic trumpet soundings are separated from the first four by means of their identification with the three  woes of chapters 8, 9, and 11. They have  come to be known by the  special title- **"The Three Woes"**, because of their severity.

John looks and hears, "*an eagle (angel) that was flying in mid-air call out in a loud voice: Woe! Woe! Woe to the inhabitants of the earth, because of the trumpet blasts about to be sounded by the other three angels!*"

The word "angel" which occurs in many translations should be translated "eagle." An eagle is sometimes pictured as God's instrument of judgment (Deut.28:49; Hosea 8:1). Thus we see that God will use even the animal kingdom for His purposes in judgment.

We note that this marks the last of three occasions on which creatures speak, as recorded in the Bible. { serpent- Gen.3:1-5; ass- Num.22:30}

# The Seven SEALS, TRUMPETS, and BOWLS Judgments of Revelation

| First Seal | Second Seal | Third Seal | Fourth Seal | Fifth Seal | Sixth Seal | Seventh Seal |
|---|---|---|---|---|---|---|
| White Horse | Red Horse | Black Horse | Pale Horse | Tribulation Saints | Great Cosmic Disturbances | Introduces The Seven Trumpets |
| Deception | War | Famine | Death | Victory | Judgment -- | ........ |
| Revelation 6:1-2 | Revelation 6:3-4 | Revelation 6:5-6 | Revelation 6:7-8 | Revelation 6:9-11 | Revelation 6:12-17 | Revelation 8:1 |

| First Trumpet | Second Trumpet | Third Trumpet | Fourth Trumpet | Fifth Trumpet | Sixth Trumpet | Seventh Trumpet |
|---|---|---|---|---|---|---|
| One third of the trees and all the grass burned up | One third of the sea becomes blood, one third of sea creatures die, one third of ships destroyed | One third of the fresh water streams become polluted | One third of the sun, moon, stars darkened | Mankind tormented for five months by spirit creatures -- THE FIRST WOE -- | One third of the remainder of mankind killed by unnatural demonlike evil spirits - THE SECOND WOE- | Introduces the Seven Bowl Judgments -- THE THIRD WOE -- |
| Revelation 8:7 | Revelation 8:8-9 | Revelation 8:10-11 | Revelation 8:12 | Revelation 9:1-12 | Revelation 9:13-21 | Revelation 11:15 |

| First Bowl | Second Bowl | Third Bowl | Fourth Bowl | Fifth Bowl | Sixth Bowl | Seventh Bowl |
|---|---|---|---|---|---|---|
| Sores on those who accepted the mark of the beast | Sea turns to blood, and all sea creatures die | Fresh water rivers turn to blood | Sun scorches humanity with great heat. Mankind curses God | The Antichrist's (Beast's) seat of government afflicted | Euphrates River dries up, to allow the world's armies to gather at Armageddon | Great Earthquakes and hail rain down on the earth |
| Revelation 16:2 | Revelation 16:3 | Revelation 16:4-7 | Revelation 16:8-9 | Revelation 16:10-11 | Revelation 16:12-16 | Revelation 16:17-21 |

# Chapter 8

---

# The Three Woes
## of
# Tribulation Judgment

The last three trumpets are separated from the other four by their identification with the three woes:

**1.** Fifth Trumpet   - First Woe:    Rev.8:13
**2.** Sixth Trumpet   - Second Woe: Rev.9:12
**3.** Seventh Trumpet - Third Woe:    Rev.11:14

These woes mark the deepest darkness and the most painful intensity of the Great Tribulation.

### 1. The Fifth Trumpet: 9:1-11

When the fifth angel sounded his trumpet, John saw "*a star fall from the sky to the earth.*" Whenever possible we should always seek to interpret words in the book of Revelation literally. However, the use of the word **"star"** in this particular reference is obviously intended figuratively rather than literally. This star is referred to as a **"him"**, thus clearly possessing personality.

There are a number of Bible students who suggest that this fallen "star" may be a fallen angel, possibly Satan himself (Isa. 14:12-15). God referred to angels as stars (Job 38:7).

This star or angel was given the keys to the bottomless pit (abyss), the abode of the demons. We note that Satan will be bound with chains and thrown into the bottomless pit during the thousand years Millennial Reign of Jesus Christ.

### The Bottomless Pit

The bottomless pit is literally, in the Greek, "the pit of the abyss," or "shaft of the abyss." It is not hell or hades. It has been suggested that it may be located at the bottom of the great gulf fixed in hades. This separates the place of torment from the place of comfort(Paradise), described as the abode of the dead by the Lord Jesus in Luke 16:19-31.

After Christ died upon the cross, He went to Paradise - the holding place of all the Old Testament saints(Lk.23:43). He then released them and took them to His Father in Heaven ( Eph.4:7-9). Today, in the church age, all believers who are truly born again do not go to Paradise when they die. Paradise today is empty. All believers go directly to be with Jesus in Heaven (2 Cor.5:1-10). All non-believers go to hell or hades which is the holding place where they wait the Great White Throne Judgment at the end of the Millennium.

The word **"shaft"** would indicate that there is an entrance from the surface of the earth to the heart of our planet. It is in this chapter that we learn for the first time of a place called the bottomless pit.

God mentions it no less than seven times in the book of Revelation (9:1,2,11; 11:7; 17:8; 20:1-3).

The identity of these demons has raised some interesting discussions throughout the ages. Some have identified them with the sons of God in Genesis 6:1,2. They say that these demons attempted sexual relations with women, resulting in immediate confinement to the bottomless pit. We do know there are two types of demons:

**1. Chained demons**          (Jude 1:7,7; 2 Pet.2:4; 1 Pet.3:18-20). Revelation 9:14 tells us that there are today bound demons held in the Euphrates River who are being kept, "*for an hour.. day... month...year,*" to be released to kill a third of mankind.

**2. Unchained Demons**          (Lk.4:34; Matt.8:29; Lk.8:27-31). These demons are free to roam the world, seeking to possess mankind as agents of the devil. The devil is not omnipresent like the Triune God, so therefore can only be at one place at any one time. He must use his fallen angels as workers to report on the world-wide activity of man.

The one who releases these demons - this fallen star mentioned in 9:1 , appears to be Satan himself. {Refer Isa.14:12; Lk.10:18; 2 Cor. 11:14). Prior to this time Christ had held the key to the bottomless pit (Rev.1:18), but now allows Satan the devil to use it for the specific purpose -  to bring judgment upon unrepentant mankind.

As Satan opens the bottomless pit, smoke

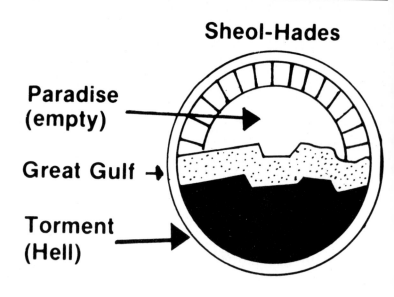

## Sheol-Hades

**Paradise (empty)**

**Great Gulf →**

**Torment (Hell)**

arises out of the pit until the air becomes saturated with a smoglike condition worse than any city has ever experienced. Out of this smog will come locust-like scorpion creatures. Interestingly enough, today we see similar creatures being created for the movie screen by the producers of science fiction films.

These locusts with supernatural power will go forth to hurt men that do not have the seal of God on their forehead. They will sting men for five months during which time they will seek death but will not find it. They will be kept alive to face this suffering. They will be led by the king of the demons whose name in the Hebrew is Abaddon, but in the Greek he is called Apollyon.

There have been many suggestion by well meaning scholars as to what these creatures represent. Furthermore, many students of prophecy mistakenly believe that they must place an interpretation on every vision and symbol in the Book of Revelation. In this particular vision we cannot intepret the scene literally, nor symbolically, but rather spiritually. The vision depicts spirit creatures, the likes of which have never been seen. If men could see them today, no doubt their hearts would fail them for fear.

These spirit creatures are released upon the earth for the express purpose of persecuting men who either have not made a decision to follow Christ (did not have the seal of God on their foreheads), or have outwardly rejected the Messiah and followed the Antichrist. The persecution they inflict upon mankind is beyond our comprehension.

## 2. The Sixth Trumpet: 9:12-21

The sounding of the sixth trumpet ushers in the second invasion of four special satanic angels. These fallen angels called demons were bound in the Euphrates River in modern-day Iraq.

This is a judgment of death. Unlike the previous trumpet judgment in which people were tormented and could not die (9:6), under the sixth trumpet a third of mankind will perish.

John continues to write: "... *I heard a voice coming from the horns of the golden altar that is before God...... Release the four angels who are bound in the great river Euphrates. And the four angels who had been kept for this very hour...day... month...year were released to kill a third of mankind. The number of the mounted troops was two hundred million."*

Again we are confronted with a measure of difficulty in interpretation. But as previously stated, we should always view each passage literally unless it is obvious that we should do otherwise. If the passage makes commonsense we should seek no other sense: otherwise it may become nonsense.

An army of 200 million men would not only present major difficulties in controlling, but also opposing. By normal standards this mighty army would occupy a territory some one kilometer in width by 200 kilometers long.

But the Scripture is quite clear in its description. This evil army of 200 million horse-like creatures are not humans that come from the eastern countries such as China. Horseman do not wear fiery red breastplates. Nor do the heads of horses resemble the heads of lions, nor do they emit from out of their mouths *"fire, smoke, and sulphur, with tails like snakes whose heads inflict injury."* Instead this is a literal description of unnatural demonlike evil spirits that come out of the abyss. They constitute a great army advancing under the leadership of the four evil angels.

### The Euphrates River

The source of this invasion is the Euphrates River. This is where the first civilization was formed (Eden - Gen.2:10), where the first murder was committed (Gen.4:8), where Nimrod built the mighty city of Babylon (Gen.10:10), where the first war was fought (Gen.14:14), where Satan had his headquarters, and evil spread its ugly tentacles throughout the world. Even today we see the rise of Babylon and the world's focus on the nation of Iraq in general, and the Middle East in particular.

The damage to be wrought by this invasion is beyond comprehension. A third of mankind will be killed. A fourth has already been slain under the fourth seal judgment (6:8). Now, assuming that these judgments will take place close to the turn of the century when we are told, the earth's population will number close to 6 billion, this could mean that after allowing for the Rapture of million of believers, and the destruction of vast numbers in the Divine judgments, only about half of the original number of people will remain on the earth during the final stages of the Tribulation Period.

## What are the results of this invasion?

The Bible says that the men who were were not killed by these plagues refused to repent of their sins. They hardened their hearts to the things of God. Jeremiah the prophet reminds us that "*The heart is deceitful above all things and beyond cure. Who can understand it ?*"

John also tells us that that these survivors would not repent of their various sins:

1. Demon worship     4. Sorcery
2. Idolatry          5. Fornication
3. Murder            6. Thefts

This seems to be a most unusual situation, where men choose to follow Satan who tortures them, rather than turn to God who loves them.

The world's troubles do not end with chapter nine. One final trumpet plague - the third woe - yet remains. This woe is recorded in chapter 11.

### 3. The Seventh Trumpet: 11:15-19

> "*And the seventh angel sounded his trumpet, and there were loud voices in heaven, which said, The kingdom of this world has become the kingdom of our Lord and of his Christ, and he will reign for ever and ever.*"

The blowing of the seventh trumpet, which is the third woe, does not initiate anything on earth. Instead, just like the breaking of the seventh seal of Revelation 8:1, it merely introduces the next series of judgments - the seven bowls.

The angel does proclaim the glorious news that very soon the Lord Jesus Christ will take over the nations of this world as their rightful ruler. As a result of this announcement, a twofold reaction is produced

**1.** The citizens of heaven rejoice; and
**2.** The nations of the earth become angry.

We are also given a clue when Christ might call the believers before the Judgment Seat of Christ in Heaven. Verse 18 says,"...*The time has come for judging the dead, and rewarding your servants the prophets and your saints and those who reverence your name ...*" In the context of this verse, the dead refers to the "dead in Christ" (1 Thess.4:16).

# Chapter 9

# Three Major Events of the Interlude

Between chapter 10:1 and 11:14 we have an interlude, a time-out period between the sixth and seventh trumpet judgments and similar to the one between the sixth and seventh seal judgments.

Three significant events take place within these chapters:

**1.** The Message of the Mighty Angel;
**2.** The Measuring of the Temple; and
**3.** The Ministry of the Two Witnesses of God.

## 1. The Message of the Mighty Angel:  10:1-11

The identity of this strong angel is debated by Bible students. Some believe he is Christ, but if he were Christ, he would have sworn by Himself ( refer Heb.6:13). This angel sware " *by him who lives for ever and ever*"(10:6). He may well be Michael the Archangel (refer Dan.12:1). He is probably the same angel referred to in chapters 5:2; 7:2; 8:3; and 18:2.

This angel whose appearance is far more radiant and spectatular than any human creature could ever hope to be, holds a little open scroll in his hand.

## What is the identity of this scroll?

Several suggestions have been made as to the identity of the book or scroll. Some believe it to be the seven-sealed book of Revelation chapter 5. Others feel it is the book mentioned in Daniel 12:9. A further idea is that the little scroll is the new revelation to John of future events, from this point on to chapter 19.

The fact is that it is a scroll, and we do know that its contents refers to events that are to come upon the earth.

## The mighty angel performs two tasks:

**1.** He firstly announces that there will be no further delay in God's judgment upon the earth: "*..... and the mystery of God is to be accomplished*".

This word "mystery" occurs several times in the Bible, meaning that God is going to disclose a truth that is only revealed in the Word of God. Man's wisdom cannot deduce these truths apart from the Word of God.

"**The mystery of God**" referred to in this chapter can only mean salvation. On earth the Christian can only experience imperfect salvation. We have the indwelling of the Spirit as a deposit guaranteeing what is to come (2 Cor.5:5). When we reach heaven our imperfect salvation becomes immediately perfect. The mystery is why such a Holy and Righteous God could love sinful men sufficiently to send His only Son into the world to die for their sins!

**2.** Secondly, he instructs John to consume the little "black" book, predicting that it would be sweet to taste, but bitter to swallow into the belly.

**What does this mean?**

The picture of sweetness in the mouth and bitterness in the belly indicates the typical quality of the Word of God. The sweetness comes to John in the sure word of the prophecy of our Lord's return. The bitterness comes in the reality of the judgments according to those same prophecies, judgments that are to come upon the earth.

Up to this point John had seen the first part of the Tribulation and it had been sweet indeed to witness ungodly Gentiles receiving their punishment. But now he is about to preview the last half of the Tribulation Judgments which will directly affect his people - the Jews. He is about to see the Antichrist stop the Temple Sacrifices, and to engage in the wholesale slaughter of Jewish citizens. This was indeed bitter medicine to him.

## 2. The Measuring of the Temple of God: 11:1,2.

Chapter 11 focuses on the spiritual life of Israel. We are told that Israel will rebuild the Temple on Mount Moriah and revert to the Old Testament form of worship. They will again introduce sacrifices because they do not believe their Messiah has already come.

Sad to say, the Jews will build this Temple in unbelief, and because of this they will be judged by the Gentiles. The Antichrist will stop the Temple Sacrifices in the middle of the Tribulation, and from this point on in God's time scale, the Jew will suffer great persecution until the Messiah returns, and then "....*all Israel will be saved*" (Rom.11:25).

## History of the Jewish Temple

There are five (5) Temples to be built in Jerusalem. Three are in the past, one is in the present, and one is future.

### 1. Solomon's Temple.

King David was the man who initiated the building project for the first Temple in Jerusalem. He originally bought the threshing-floor from Araunah the Jebusite (2 Sam.24:24) but David was not allowed by God to physically commence the building because he was a man of war. David's son Solomon built the Temple in seven years, and it became known as Solomon's Temple.

The Shekinah Glory of God appeared in the Temple at Jerusalem and became a symbol of the protecting hand of God upon the nation of Israel.

Despite the warnings of the prophets of impending judgment, the people continued to disobey God's laws. They forsook His ways for the pleasures of their pagan neighbours. The northern ten tribes fell captive to the Assyrians in 721 B.C. The southern kingdom of Judah thought itself impregnable as long as the Temple stood. They shut their ears to the cries of Jeremiah and Ezekiel.

After three campaigns commencing in 606 B.C., the Babylonian king Nebuchadnezzar finally sacked Jerusalem and destroyed the Temple in 586 B.C. and at that point a chapter had closed in Israel's history.

### 2. Zerubbabel's Temple

Seventy years after the first campaign by king

Nebuchadnezzar against Jerusalem, a decree was issued to rebuild the city and eventually the Temple. The construction of this Temple was under the direction of Zerubbabel and Joshua, the high priest.

This second Temple was much inferior to the first Temple. That was made clear when the elders, who remembered the glory of Solomon's Temple, wept when they saw the foundations of this new Temple. The Temple became the focal point of life in an increasing hostile environment. It served the people well until it was desecrated by Antiochus Epiphanes, one of the Greco-Syrian rulers, in 174 B.C.

This abomination that causes desolation as predicted by Daniel 7:13 is a fore-runner of that which will happen during the reign of the Antichrist in the rebuilt Temple in Jerusalem. Jesus also predicted its destruction in Matthew 24:15.

### 3. Herod's Temple

The Romans conquered Jerusalem under the leadership of Pompey in the year 64 B.C. About forty years before the birth of Christ, Herod the Great, so named because of his massive building program, had the deteriorated Temple destroyed and completly rebuit on an enlarged scale. It was in Herod's Temple that Jesus attended the Passover at the age of twelve years. It was just outside the walls of the city containing the Temple where Jesus was crucified for the sins of mankind some twenty years later.

Jesus predicted that this Temple would be destroyed, and not one stone would be left upon another (Matt. 24:2). This prophecy was fulfilled in the year AD.70 when Titus the Roman general laid seige to the city of Jerusalem. Although he gave orders that the Temple should not be destroyed, the Jews burned it rather than allow it to fall into pagan hands.

The prophecy that Jesus gave on the Mount of Olives has been fulfilled in every detail. Today the only evidence we find remaining from Herod's era are the huge stone blocks seen at the base of the Temple Mount, known as the Western or Wailing Wall. These stones were not from the Temple but were part of the outer wall of Herod's Temple. Titus commanded his soldiers to leave these huge stone blocks as a memorial to the building achievements of the Romans.

The Moslem mosque located on the Temple Mount - known as the "Dome of the Rock" - is made of entirely different building material from that with which Herod's Temple was constructed.

### 4. The Tribulation Temple

Ever since the Jews have returned to their land and declared nationhood status in 1948, there have been plans to rebuild the Temple in Jerusalem on the exact site of Solomon's Temple.

The one piece of land that the Jews want more than any other is the site occupied in part by the Dome of the Rock. Considering the current political climate, it is unlikely the Moslems will allow a Jewish Temple to be built.

Recent activity among fundamental Jews regarding Temple rebuilding indicates a definite sign that the coming of Jesus Christ is indeed close.

## When will the Temple be Rebuilt?

That the temple must be rebuilt there is no argument. If the Jews had their way it would have been completed years ago. When the Israel armed forces took over Jerusalem during the War of Liberation in 1967, the then defence minister, Moshe Dayan could have placed control of the Temple mount under the Israel government. He chose to leave control of this highly sensitive area in the hands of Arabs. **Why?**

The answer is relatively simple. It was not the right timing in God's calendar. But the Temple will be rebuilt, and that time is almost now.

According to the prophecy in Daniel 9:27, for the Antichrist to stop the sacrifices and offering in the middle of the Tribulation, the Temple must be built by at least the mid-point of the Tribulation Period:

*"He will confirm a covenant with many for one seven (seven years), but in the middle of that seven (after three and one half years), he will put an end to sacrifice and offering....."*

The act of signing this covenant or peace pact with Israel by the Antichrist commences the time known as the Tribulation period. This ungodly association by the Jews with the Antichrist will also permit them to commence the building program for the Temple, and once again to institute the sacrificial system.

When this is done it will be yet another rejection of Christ by God's chosen people. However, God will judge them again by allowing the

Antichrist to set up an image in the Temple, and bring a halt to the sacrificial system.

## Measuring the Temple

The fact that John was told to go and measure the Temple is a good indication that he would find this Tribulation one, drawn to man's specification, totally inadequate compared to Solomon's Temple, which was inspired by God.

John was also told not to measure the outer court area because it had been given over to the Gentiles. This seems to indicate that the Jewish authorities will control only the area immediately surrounding the location of the newly constructed Temple.

Furthermore, there is also the indication that the Dome of the Rock, which is not built over the site of Solomon's Temple, but 100 meters to the south, could remain in its present location. The two structures could co-exist, and not be in conflict with the word of prophecy.

### 5. The Millennial Temple

This is the last Temple to be built on earth. Its plans are detailed in Ezekiel chapters 40 to 48. The architect is God, and when His son Jesus returns to earth He will personally supervise its construction.

This Temple will be the centre of worship during the Millennial Reign of Jesus Christ, and will be located in the middle of the New Jerusalem - a city 55 square kilometers.

Other references to this Temple are found in Joel 3:18; Isa.2:3; 60:13; Dan.9:24; Haggai 2:7,9.

## 3. The Ministry of the Two Witnesses: 11:3-13

The suffering of the Tribulation continues. We now see two witnesses come to earth from heaven to proclaim the message of hope amidst the judgments of God. Despite their message, they are not accepted. Sin despises righteousness and godly warnings and teachings. Although men know that the Rapture will have already taken place, they will not change their attitudes toward God.

John hears an angelic spokesman say the following about these two individuals:

*"And I will give power to my two witnesses, and they will prophesy for 1260 days, clothed in sackcloth"*

If we allow a prophetic year to have 12 months of 30 days each, as it is in the Old Testament, the two witnesses would be carrying out their warning messages for $3\frac{1}{2}$ years. This is exactly half of the seven years Tribulation Period.

During their witness, the Holy City of Jerusalem is under the control of foreign armies. The time of this control is stated as being 42 months (Rev. 13:5), or exactly $3\frac{1}{2}$ years.

The purpose of these two witnesses is that God must protect his people the Jews during this time or they will suffer intense persecution. The period of protection lasts for "a time, and times, and half a time" (Rev 12:14). If a "time" equals one year, we again have a period of $3\frac{1}{2}$ years: a time + two times + half a time.

## The Identity of the Two Witnesses

God has not seen fit to tell us who the two great witnesses to the Jewish people might be. On this basis we can only speculate as to their identity. Some of the most reliable suggestions are:

**1. Elijah and Enoch.** Hebrews 9:27 states that all men are appointed to die once, and since these two men did not experience physical death, they will be sent back to witness and eventually each would die a martyr's death.

**2. Elijah.** Malachi 4:5,6 predicts that God will send Elijah during that great and dreadful day of the Lord (refer also Matt.17:11). Elijah also appeared with the glorified Christ on the Mount of Transfiguration.

**3. Moses.** In the Book of Jude verse 9, we are informed that after the death of Moses, Satan attempted to acquire his dead body, so that God would not be able to use him against the Antichrist during the Tribulation. Moses also appeared with Christ on the Mount of Transfiguration.

**4. Elijah and Moses.** Elijah represents the prophets, and Moses the Law. During their earthly ministry both men performed a number of miracles.

In the case of Elijah he called fire down from heaven, and also shut up the sky from raining for three years. Moses turned the waters in Egypt into blood, and brought many plagues upon that land. Each of the miracles performed by Elijah and Moses will again be repeated by the witnesses during the Tribulation Period.

## What is their Ministry?

**a)** To prophesy for $3\frac{1}{2}$ years before men in the Holy City as God's anointed lampstands;

**b)** If they are attacked for their testimony,to destroy their enemies with fire;

**c)** To prevent rain for three and one half years;

**d)** To turn water into blood;

**e)** To smite the earth with every kind of plague as often as is necessary.

## The Witnesses' Death and Resurrection

After three and one half years of preaching, the Beast that comes out of the bottomless pit kills the witnesses. This is the same Beast as in Revelation 13:1-7, and the fact that he comes out of the "Abyss" is a clear reference to the death and resurrection of the Antichrist, as we will see in more detail when we consider chapter 13 of Revelation.

The Antichrist, in showing contempt for the two witnesses, will refuse permission for their bodies to be buried, but will leave them to rot in the streets of Jerusalem. All the earth (now possible through satellite television) will celebrate their deaths in a "Hellish" Christmas. Their bodies will be displayed in the streets of this once Holy City, now figuratively called Sodom and Egypt.

Jerusalem is referred to as Sodom because of its immorality, and as Egypt because of the worldliness of its people.

We note that this is the only reference to **_rejoice_** throughout the entire Tribulation.

## The Rapture of the Witnesses

As the church will enjoy a triumphant Rapture, so will the two super witnesses. After the three and half days in front of the whole world which gloats to see them dead, suddenly the *"spirit of life from God will enter them, and they will stand on their feet."* They will hear the voice of God calling from heaven saying, *"Come up here,"* and they will disappear in a cloud - in a similar manner whereby Jesus ascended from the Mount of Olives 2000 years ago.

No wonder *"great terror"* will strike the crowd as they look on. This will be the first time the television cameras will be ready to capture a translation. The world will not know when the Rapture of the believers will occur. That event is imminent. It could happen at any time. But this spectacle will be different, for the timing will be precise, to the very hour.

The resurrection of these men will be the final confirmation that they were holy men sent from God. As a result, some will fear God and give Him glory. In fact, we read of a great earthquake that destroyed a tenth of the city, killing seven thousand people. Maybe as a result of this cataclysmic judgment of God upon Jerusalem, a tide of revival will sweep across Israel during the latter half of the Tribulation Period. Certainly we are told that a revival will occur among the survivors as a result of this devastation (Rev.11:13; Joel 2:28-32).

# Chapter 10

---

# Satan Versus Israel

Chapters 12 and 13 of Revelation introduce us to a major religious and spiritual struggle. The apostle Paul warned in his letter to the church at Ephesus, *"For our struggle is not against flesh and blood, but against the rulers, against the authorities, against the powers of this dark world and against the spiritual forces of the evil in the heavenly realms"* (Eph.6:12).

Chapter 12 focuses our attention on the nation of Israel. We should never be surprised that so much attention is directed to this relatively small insignificant nation, located in one of the most arid and desolate regions of the world. She dominates the pages of the Old Testament because she is God's nation of destiny.

It is because of God's love for Israel that Satan now launches all the power he can muster in an all-out effort to annihilate God's chosen - "the apple of His eye."

Satan is the craftiest of all of God's creation. We should never underestimate him. He has great power to perform supernatural acts. His plan has been and always will be to destroy. He deceives by changing his personality, and he never gives up. He seeks to destroy all that is of God. He is the master mimic, and will display that attribute during his reign of terror for seven years.

This chapter in Revelation really commences with the last verse of chapter 11. John sees the Temple and the Ark of the Covenant in heaven. Both the Ark and the Temple are of central concern to Israel. Archeologists have been digging among the ruins of Jerusalem and elsewhere in Israel for centuries, looking for the lost Ark of the Covenant. From this scene we may possibly deduce that the original Ark of the Covenant was always located in the Temple in Heaven. Only a copy made by man was located in the Temple built by Solomon.
(Refer: Isa.6:1-8; Ex.25:9; Heb.8:2,5; 9:24; Rev.15:5.)

## Satan's Final Attack from Heaven

The picture of the woman clothed with the sun, moon, and a crown of twelve stars, represents Israel as a nation. As the sun, moon, and stars are light-conveying objects - the sun being the source, the moon and the stars the reflectors, so too was Israel to be God's light-bearers to a lost world. However, over the years the sins of the nation have dimmed their radiance, but once again in these last days a small number will rekindle the flame in the form of the 144,000 witnesses.

It is interesting to compare the church in all this. According to the messages of Revelation 2 and 3, the church is God's "lampstand" to get His message out in <u>this</u> generation.

This woman which represents the nation of Israel, the nation which gave birth to Christ (Refer:Isa,9:6; Micah 5:2-3), is seen having a crown with twelve stars, representative of the twelve tribes of Israel. The child she is about to give birth to is none other than a reference to Jesus Christ.

Another sign now appears in heaven.The red dragon symbolizes Satan the devil, with 7 heads and 10 horns. The seven heads are a symbol of the seven empires that proceed the kingdom of Christ The ten horns are a symbol of earthly power. "*His tail sweeps a third of the stars out of the sky*," is an obvious reference to the original fall of one third of the angels who rebelled with Lucifer and was cast to earth.   The whole purpose of Satan's mission is to destroy the male child - Jesus Christ.

This is not the first time that Satan has attempted to destroy the Saviour of the world after the pronouncement of his doom by God in the Garden of Eden( Gen.3:15),  Satan tried to stop the seed by the murder of Abel by Cain (Gen.4); by his attempts to captivate the Hebrew nation in Egypt (Ex.1,2); by the decree of Haman (Esther 3:8-15); and by Herod's decree to kill babies in Israel (Matt.2:13).

## Satan's Titles

There is no question as to the identity  of the red dragon of chapter 12. Verse 9 tells us that it is Satan. But why is he called by so many names? He is given at least seven (7) in this chapter alone:

**1. The great red dragon** (12:3). Great, because of his power. Red, because he was the first murderer. Dragon, because of his viciousness.

**2. The old serpent** (12:9). Old, because of his activities in the garden of Eden (Gen.3); Serpent - it reminds us of the first body he used (Gen.3).

**3. The devil** (12:9). It means one who slanders (Job.1,2; Zech.3:1-7; Lk. 22:31).

**4. Satan** (12:9). This meaning of his name is adversary (1 Pet.5:8).

**5. The deceiver** (12:9). We should note that he not only deceives men, but also angels (Acts 14:9).

**6. The persecutor** (12:4) This is a reference to his role of using Herod and the Romans to kill the child.

**7. The hater of Christ** (12:5). This verse tells us of Christ's birth, ascension, and future reign. Satan would be absolutely wild and uncontrollable knowing of his ultimate defeat by Christ.

   **Note:** It is important to be aware when studying the prophetic word that often history jumps millenniums in just one verse of Scripture. Sometimes that movement is forward, at other times it may be backwards. In chapter 12:4 there is a jump in time within the verse of 4000 years. In verse five, the time advances 2000 years and then backwards 2000 years.

   The best example is found in Isaiah 65:17-18. Verse 17 speaks about the Eternal state. Verse 18 jumps backwards 2000 years to speak about the Millennial Reign of Christ on this present earth.

## Where did Israel go to ecsape the Antichrist?

Verse 6 and verses 13-16  tells us that,"*The woman fled into the desert to a place prepared for her by God, where she might be taken care of for 1260 days.*"

In the eleventh chapter of the book of Daniel we are given a graphic picture of a world war raging in the Middle East involving many nations under the control of the Antichrist. We are also told that during these last days when the king of the south and the king of the north are challenging the authority of the Antichrist who has invaded the "beautiful land", the country of Jordan will appear to remain neutral and present a safe haven for Israel.

During these terrible last days, Israel will flee across the Dead Sea into Jordan, or more specifically to the area known as Petra which is the ancient land of Edom. (refer. Matt.24:16-20).  Petra today is a rock fortress located 200 kms south of Amman, the capital of Jordan, and about 150 kms south- east of Jerusalem. The area is a labyrinth of caves in one of the most mountainous areas on the Arabian Peninsula.

Apparently those who choose to flee the invading forces of the Antichrist surrounding Jerusalem will be protected by God in this mountainous region ( Rev.12:13-17).

When Christ returns at the Second Coming, He will first go to Edom or Petra to rescue the Jews, while at the same time He will destroy the forces of the Antichrist (Isa. 63:1-6).

### The War in Heaven

It has been suggested that this war in heaven it not just a single battle, but rather a continual struggle of good versus evil. Whatever the situation was in the past, we now witness one final thrust by Satan and his demons to usurp the authority of God. The result of the spiritual battle with Michael and his angels is defeat for Satan, because he is finally cast out of heaven forever.

One question often asked is, "If Satan fell from heaven just before or at the time of creation, how is it that he still has access to the heavenly realm?"

We are told in this chapter that Satan is the great accuser of God's people (v.10). Job chapter 1 indicates that Satan can roam to and fro throughout the world gathering information on people to report to God. In order to achieve his function, I believe Satan has been given limited access to heaven, probably being allowed to enter a judical chamber only for the express purpose of presenting these accusations before God.

He would never be allowed to enter the inner sanctuary of heaven at any time. He lost that privilege when Lucifer the shining light became Satan the adversary.

As a result of Satan's demise out of Heaven, there is great rejoicing. God can now proceed with His plans for the future without the distraction of the evil one. However, the earth will now mourn because Satan is about to vent his full fury on all of the remaining faithful to God( Rev.13:17).

# Chapter 11

# The Two Beasts: Antichrist and the False Prophet

Revelation chapter 13 introduces to the world two personages well known to students of Bible prophecy. We are told by what means Satan makes war against the faithful of God's people who now see that the only way to heaven is martyrdom. If only they had been prepared before the rapture!

We are also given a graphic picture of how Satan attempts to control the world through the eyes of the Antichrist and the False Prophet.

The term **"Beast"** in Revelation can refer to a government or world power, or to one of the world's rulers. In Revelation 11:7 we learn of a ruler who put to death God's two prophets. This ruler is called the "Beast who is rising from the Abyss." This language hints at why there are earlier versions of antichrist as well as the final and most diabolical one. Moral evil is always seeking to break out of the Abyss and take over the earth. However, God so controls our world that antichrists do not last long. This will be true also of the final Antichrist who is about to step into the arena of world events.

# The Difference between the Two Beasts

**The First Beast** of Revelation chapter 13:1-10 is the diabolical figure known as **The Antichrist.** The following gives some idea as to his background and activity during the Tribulation.

**1.   He arose out of the Sea.** The word "sea" is used in this context to mean that the Antichrist arises from among the people around the Mediterranean Sea.

**2.   He has 7 heads and 10 horns.** The seven heads are seven mountains, which also symbolize seven kings dominated by the harlot Babylon (idolatry-Rev.17:9).   The ten horns of Revelation 17:12 are the ten kings who will make up the Antichrist's world confederacy of nations.

**3.   His head is adorned with names of blasphemy.**

**4.   He will have a beast-like nature.**   This dictator's movement onto the world scene will be fast (leopard); he will be powerful (bear); he will be a distinguished person (lion).

**5.   He will be worshipped.** This world leader will claim to have been fatally wounded; will fake a resurrection; the world will be absolutely amazed; and this will cause people to worship him and Satan (v4).   Open satanic worship will characterize the "church" of the Tribulation.

**6.   He makes war with the saints and wins.**

**7.   His activities are for 42 months.**

**8.   He is finally destroyed by the Lamb.** He goes into perdition, and is finally cast into the lake of fire (Rev.19:20).

**The Second Beast** of Revelation chapter 11: 11-18 is known as **The False Prophet**

**1.    He is the Beast out of the Earth.** Alongside the first beast - Antichrist -  Biblical prophecy places a person who will serve him as a sort of religious front man, a false prophet, a henchman to force the people into worshipping Antichrist.

**2.    He will have great influence.**    He will be the dictator's right-hand support.  He will be the religious arm to the political leadership of the Antichrist - a real False Prophet.

**3.    He will display awesome power.** This pyrotechnic "cleric" will deceive millions into believing that he can save the world, which by now will be bursting at the seams.

**4.    He will set up a 'live' image of Antichrist.** It is amazing how history tends to repeat itself. Nebuchadnezzar had an image set up in Babylon's main city square and demanded that it be worshipped. The False Prophet will demand that people worship this image which has powers of speech. Could it not be computer controlled?

**5.    He will control the economy of the day.** The beast will have a mark prepared (666) that people will be required to wear on their right arm or forehead. Having this mark will be their passport to buy or sell during his reign.

There is good news for the believers. We will not experience this terrifying future. During the beast's rampage on earth, Christians will be in Heaven enjoying fellowship with Jesus Christ.

# What is the Mark of the Beast?

The mark of the Beast is discussed exclusively in Revelation 13:16-18.   It has captured the imagination of mankind even to the extent that there are many people today who read a 666 on the Australian Bankcard, and because of this will not have anything to do with credit charging.

**What then is this mark?**     It is the mark of a system headed by the Antichrist, used to identify all people during the Tribulation Period who worship and follow the Beast.

### Believers will not have to worry.

Scripture is very clear about the mark. It is to be borne either on the forehead or in the palm of the right hand. It will be administered by the False Prophet only from the half way point during the Tribulation - i.e., after three and one half years of the seven years of Tribulation.

People alive during the Tribulation will need to make a choice. The moment they take the mark, they seal their fate. There can be **no salvation** for those people who take the mark of the Beast.

**What does this number mean?**     The Bible says in Revelation 13:18, " *If anyone has insight, let him calculate the number of the Beast, for it is a man's number.*" In general, most scholars agree that the number **6** as applied to Scripture represents Man. (Man was created on the 6th day: 6 days were alloted for man to work.)

Seven denotes completeness, but six implies incompleteness, always falling short.   Now, as the Holy Trinity (Father, Son, Holy Spirit) is the embodiment of Godliness, so the embodiment of evil is manifested in a counterfeit trinity - **Satan, Antichrist, and the False Prophet.**

It may also be that the beast will use the "**6**" three times to emulate the Godhead!

## Who is this Antichrist?

It is quite Scriptural to apply wisdom to calculate the number of the Beast (Rev. 13:18), but nowhere have we the authority to name him. We are not privy to his name. That will be revealed in God's timing and, as we have already indicated, according to Paul's letter to the Thessalonians the Antichrist cannot be revealed while the church is still on the earth.

Unfortunately there are many well-meaning people and groups who spend all their energies endeavouring to implicate different people. Hitler has been a candidate. More recent thinking has suggested that Saddam Hussein from Iraq could be a likely candidate. The current Pope who is known as the "Vicar of Christ" is a popular target. Using letters from the Latin Alphabet which have numerical values, his title *"Vicarius Filii Dei"* is made to add up to **666.**

Surely we would do better to forget the fantasy and concentrate on the reality of God's Word!

## Contrast between Christ and Antichrist

| Christ | Antichrist |
| --- | --- |
| 1. Christ came from above - Jn. 6:38 | 1. Antichrist will ascend from the pit - Rev. 11:7 |
| 2. Christ came in His Father's name - Jn. 5:43 | 2. He will come in His own name - Jn. 5:43 |
| 3. Christ humbled himself - Phil. 2:8 | 3. He will exalt himself - 2 Thess. 2:4 |
| 4. Christ was despised - Isa. 53:3; Lk. 23:18 | 4. He will be admired - Rev.13:3,4 |
| 5. Christ will be exalted - Phil. 2:9 | 5. He will be cast down to hell - Rev. 19:20 |
| 6. Came to do His Father's will - Jn. 6:38 | 6. He will come to do his own will - Dan. 11:36 |
| 7. Christ came to save - Lk. 19:10 | 7. He will come to destroy - Dan. 8:24 |
| 8. Christ is the good shepherd - Jn. 10:1-15 | 8. He is the "idol (evil) shepherd - Zech. 11:16 |
| 9. Christ is the "true vine" - Jn. 15:1 | 9. He is the "vine of the earth" - Rev. 14:18 |
| 10. Christ is the truth - Jn. 14:6 | 10. He is the "lie" - 2 Thess. 2:11 |
| 11. Christ is the "holy one" - Mk. 1:24 | 11. He is the "Lawless one" 2 Thess. 2:8 |
| 12. Christ is the "man of sorrows" - Isa. 53:3 | 12. He is the "man of sin" - 2 Thess. 2:3 |
| 13. Christ is the "Son of God" - Lk. 1:35 | 13. He is the "son of perdition" - 2 Thess. 2:3 |
| 14. He is "the mystery of Godliness" - 1 Tim. 3:16 | 14. He will be "the mystery of iniquity" - 2 Thess. 2:7 |
| 15. He is the image of God - Jn. 14:9 | 15. He is the image of Satan - Rev. 12:3; 13:1; 17:3 |
| 16. Christ has for His Bride His church, holy and blameless, which He will raise with Him in glory. - Eph. 5:25-27 | 16. The Antichrist has for a wife a prostitute, the apostate church, which he shall put to an end by burning - Rev. 17:1-16 |

# Chapter 12

---

# The Lull Before
## the
# Final Storm

We have already seen that two chapters in Revelation - namely 4 and 5  are given over to describing some heavenly action just prior to the fearful seal judgments which began in Revelation 6. In the next two chapters - 14 and 15 - we again have a record of a number of heavenly actions taking place before the final bowl judgments.

**Chapter 14**  briefly moves beyond the storm on earth. It looks ahead to the time when the sealed servants of God - the 144,000 Jewish evangelists- are seen resting from their labours on heavenly Mount Zion. But then the reader is brought back to the tumult and commotion on earth. God has warned the world for the last time. Whoever takes the mark of the beast - whoever is part of this world's corrupt system, is about to suffer the final wrath of God. The seven last plagues are about to ravage planet earth.

**Chapter 15** is a prologue to the last seven plagues.  *"Out of the temple came the seven angels having the seven plagues"* (Rev.15:6).

# The 144,000 and the Lamb

In the opening portion of chapter 14  the apostle John again sees a group of 144,000 people, this time standing with the Lamb on heavenly Mount Zion. These people are the same group we met in chapter 7. There they were sealed by God and sent forth to evangelize the world during the first half of the Tribulation. Now these Jewish witnesses are seen in heaven.

## How did they get to Heaven?

Put simply, they were Raptured or redeemed from the earth  in mid-Tribulation after completing their alloted task of being God's lightbearer to a lost and devastated world. They now sing a new song accompanied by heavenly harps. This group make up the greatest numbered choir of all time.

## What are their Qualifications?

**1.    They were morally pure**- v.4  "*They did not defile themselves with women for they kept themselves pure.*"  Interpretation of this statement has presented some difficulty over the centuries. A number of scholars say that this group consists of unmarried men. However, nowhere does the Bible teach that sexual intercourse in marriage is defiling. Hebrews 13:4 says,"*Marriage should be honoured by all, and the marriage kept pure, for God will judge the adulterer and all the sexually immoral.*"

It would appear that what this passage is saying is that these 144,000 did not allow themselves to be influenced  by sexual pleasures during their ministry. Being high profile evangelists, it would be very easy to become distracted with the pleasures of women. How we have seen evidence of Satan's influence in this area among the tele-evangelists and others in the evangelical churches of the world!

**2.    They were Available for Service** - v.4    By today's standard this select group of evangelists were a little unusual. They were totally obedient to the call for which they were chosen.

**3.    They Tell the Truth** - v.5        Lying is a natural part of man's nature when he is captivated by Satan. One of the main characteristics of an obedient Christian is that he tells the truth.

**4.    They were Purchased as Firstfruits.** - v.4 Christ was the firstfruits of the resurrection, the first to rise from the dead, and never to die again (1 Cor. 15:20). This group are the firstfruits of the Tribulation Period, the first people to be saved during that time by virtue of the fact that they were specifically selected and sealed by God in accordance with His sovereignty.

     We note that a much larger group will also be saved during the same period (Rev.7:9).

## The Message from the Three Angels

**1.    The First Angel** - 14:6-7
     *"And I saw another angel flying in mid-air, and he had the eternal gospel to proclaim.........."*
     We see in this verse something absolutely

unique - an angel of God preaching the gospel to sinners. Angels were never commissioned to go forth to preach the everlasting gospel. That job was always the responsibility of the redeemed people of God. However, the fact that an angel will witness to the world shows:

**1.** The lateness of the hour and the urgency of the message of salvation.

**2.** That barriers regarding different language would not present a problem to a celestial being.

### What is the Everlasting Gospel?

It is the same gospel preached by the apostle Paul. It is the good news to all Tribulation believers that judgment will soon be over, and the good news to all Tribulation non-believers that escape from God's judgment through salvation in Jesus Christ is still possible.

One of the sad situations we sometimes find in churches is that people want to believe in the Lord Jesus Christ, but are not told how. Often people are asked to come forward and accept Jesus, but in the process are not told how to repent of their sins - only that they should love and accept Jesus.

When Philip preached to the Ethiopian eunuch we know he told that man the whole truth of the gospel because the first question we hear the Ethiopian asking is, *"Look here is water,: Why shouldn't I be baptised?"* (Acts 8:35).

The angel, in warning the people to fear God instead of Antichrist, also instructs then how. He says, *"... give him glory. Worship the creator."*

## 2.    The Second Angel - 14:8

"*A second angel followed and said,   Fallen! Fallen is Babylon the Great, which made all the nations drink the maddening wine of her adulteries.*"

The second message is simply to announce in advance  the imminent destruction of the political and economic Babylon, as outlined in Revelation chapter 18.   It is a blessed truth that God never brings judgment upon mankind  without advance warnings.

## 3.    The Third Angel - 14:9-12

"A *third angel followed and said, If anyone worships the beast and his image and receives his mark on the forehead or on the hand, he too will drink the wine of God's fury............. He will be tormented with burning sulphur in the presence of the holy angels and the Lamb...........There is no rest day or night for those who worship the beast and his image, or for anyone who receives the mark of his name.*"

The third angel pronounces doom on the worshippers of Antichrist during the Tribulation Period. This will be the last hell-fire and brimstone message that will ever be preached to the unsaved. Here we see that God will pour out His undiluted wrath upon mankind from which there will be no escape.

## The Blessed State of the Dead - The Linchpin

We now have in verse 13 one of the most important clues in the book of Revelation as to the activity of people who are martyred for Christ during the seven years of the Tribulation Period.

# "ACTIVITY DURING THE TRIBULATION"

## HEAVEN

Judgment Seat of Christ

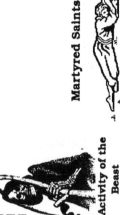

Marriage Supper of the Lamb

**Resurrection of :**

........ In Mid-Tribulation ....... }

1. Tribulation Saints
   (first 1260 days only)
2. 144,000 Jews
3. The Two Witnesses

---

**7 year Tribulation Period :-** {7x360 dys. = 2520 dys. - 3½yrs.= 1260 dys.}

## EARTH

7 year Tribulation Judgments

Activity of the Beast

Mid-Tribulation Point

Martyred Saints

Resurrected when Christ Returns

**1.   The Rapture:** The removal of all *believers* when Christ comes for His saints. Those who are left on the earth after the removal of the true church will consist of all unbelievers and carnal Christians (those who believe in a God but have never made a confession of faith - i.e., they are not truly born again. They are not Holy Spirit filled believers).

**2.   The Tribulation Period:**   This period will commence with the revelation of the Antichrist. During the first three and one half years, those who are killed for their testimony for Christ will be resurrected to heaven and will be known as *Tribulation Saints* ( Rev. 7:9-17).

At the mid-point of the Tribulation, after three and one half years, two significant events take place:

**a)**   Rapture to heaven of the 144,000 *Jewish Witnesses* (Rev.14:1).

**b)**   Rapture of the *Two Special Witnesses* in Jerusalem (Rev.11:12).

From the mid-point of the Tribulation to the end those who die in Christ are known as *Martyred Saints* but will not be resurrected at the moment of death.   Revelation 14:13 says: "...... *Blessed are the dead who die in the Lord from now on. Yes, says the Spirit, they will rest from their labour, for their deeds will follow them.*"

Apparently they will be held in a "soulish state" which could be in Paradise - the place of comfort, which today is empty. They will be raised at the Second Coming of Jesus Christ (Rev.20:4).

The immediate question that comes to mind is,

**Why?** If the first half Tribulation believers go immediately to heaven when they die, why not the second half Tribulation believers?

The answer to this question probably lies in the fact that Satan is no longer able to be our great accuser before God because he has been confined to earth about the same time - i.e., at the mid-point of the Tribulation Period. In addition, Rev.11:18 suggests that our Lord will be occupied from the mid-point of the Tribulation with the judgment in heaven (Bema judgment), and the subsequent allocation of rewards for the believers. (Note that this is NOT the judgment of the Great White Throne).

Quite apart from the actual mechanics of these Raptures and Resurrections, each special group will be blessed because they will be reigning with Christ for all Eternity.

### The Prelude to Armageddon

In verses 14 to 20 we see three more angels involved in the final judgments. This particular section is a prophetic foreglimpse of what is to come, the details of which are to be found under the bowl judgments of Revelation 16:12-16 and 19:11-20.

John sees the harvest that one day will come upon the earth, but this is not a harvest of souls as was the case in Revelation chapter 7. This is a harvest of God's wrath.

The reaper is Christ Himself, pictured sitting on a white cloud with a crown of gold on his head, symbolic of the fact that He will conquer those who will oppose Him. The time has now come to reap the harvest which is ripe for the picking.

Three angels come as instruments of God's judgment:

1. **The angel of verse 15.** This angel encourages Christ to delay no longer, but to take the sharp sickle that we saw Christ holding in verse 14, and to reap the ripe harvest. As a result of God's judgment, the earth was harvested, or the pollution caused by sin was removed, to make way for the return of Christ to earth.

2. **The angel of verse 17.** This angel is concerned about gathering the grape clusters.

3. **The angel of verse 18.** Here we have an angel who had power over fire.

All three angels work together. The Lord Himself also has a sharp sickle, and is the judge in the ultimate sense. But He chooses to use angels to help in accomplishing His purposes.

The vine is a symbol of a religious system, while the winepress is a symbol of the wrath of God which is to come. Verse 19 tells us that the angel swung his sickle to earth, gathered the clusters of grapes, and threw them into the great winepress of God's wrath.

**What was the result?** The blood flowed as high as the horses' bridles in a stream for 300 kilometres. In that day, and because of war, the entire length of Israel, which is about 300 kilometers will be one huge battlefield as the armies of the earth assemble there. It is easy to see the reality of this prophecy when we note that Revelation 16:21 indicates that hailstones weighing about 40 kilograms fall to earth. These hailstones will squash

the armies of men and, as the hail melts, great
torrents of blood and water will flow throughout the
land.

N.P. It is important to be ready to meet the
Lord when the Rapture takes place. Thank God for
making a way of escape from this terrible time of
sorrow!

### The Sights and Sounds of the Temple

Chapter 15 is the shortest in the book of
Revelation, but no less important than all the
others. The chapter serves as an introduction to the
bowl judgments of chapter 16, and reveals some
important truths concerning the wrath of God. The
Temple in heaven is opened again and we are given
another glimpse of its importance in the
administration and worship of God's heavenly
kingdom.

God's wrath continues. "*Out of the temple came
the seven angels with the seven plagues*" (v. 16). But
first John sees a "*great and marvellous sign,*" and
hears the song of the triumphal (vv. 1-4).

**1.   The Symbol:** John saw a sea of glass mixed
with fire. This may be the same sea we observed in
Revelation 4:6, representing all the redeemed out
of the first half of the Tribulation Period. However,
on the other hand it could represent all the martyred
saints of the last three and a half years of the
Tribulation who did not take the mark of the Beast.
They are not the saints of the church age, but they
are clearly believers in Jesus Christ, for otherwise

they would not be in the presence of God. Certainly the fire speaks of the suffering of the redeemed who have come out of the Tribulation.

**2.    The Song:** They sang a song of Moses and of the Lamb (v.3). Note the contrast between these songs:

**a)**    The song of Moses was sung beside the Red Sea (Ex.15); the song of the Lamb will be sung beside the crystal (glass) sea.

**b)**    The song of Moses was sung over Egypt; the song of the Lamb will be sung over Babylon.

**c)**    The song of Moses described how God brought His people out; the song of the Lamb will describe how God brings His people in.

**d)**    The song of Moses was Scripture's first song; the song of the Lamb will be Scripture's last song.

**Why do they sing?** Because God is Holy, and we should honour and respect Him. "*All nations will come and worship before Him.*" This is a prophecy referring to the Millennial Reign of Jesus Christ.

### The Temple and Tabernacle of God

The Temple is now seen open in Heaven. The Temple is referred to 15 times in the Book of Revelation. Each reference is either to the Temple in Heaven, or to the absence of the Temple in the New Jerusalem.

In the Old Testament days, Moses ministered in an earthly Tabernacle. In this chapter we see the Lord in His Heavenly Tabernacle which is again open, just as it was in Revelation 11:19. This

Temple is called the "*Tabernacle of the Testimony.*"
It may be called this because the Ten
Commandments which were kept in the ark were
later taken to the Temple.

**Who comes out of the Temple?** Now we read
about the seven angels with the seven vials of God's
final judgment upon the earth. They are all clothed
in clean shining linen, wearing golden sashes around
their chests.    This is a symbolic picture of the
purity, righteousness, and faithfullness of Almighty
God. These angels have been allocated the task of
pouring out the wrath of God upon planet earth.

The introduction to the final judgments closes
with the Temple of God being *"filled with smoke
from the glory of God and from his power."*

God has never promised to remove all of man's
sufferings and sorrows. Because God is Holy, He
must judge in order that the world may know of
this holiness and greatness. However, He does give
mankind strength to endure suffering with a right
attitude of heart when called upon. But the age-old
question still nags, "Why do the righteous suffer?"
This can be answered only by God, and God alone.
The child of God does, however, have the assurance
that there is a purpose for his suffering, and that
God is exercising His will in their life. The non-
believer on the other hand will get no help during
his or her time of suffering.

# Chapter 13

# The Seven Vials of God's Wrath

The entire 16th chapter of Revelation describes a horrendous series of natural catastropes emanating from the hand of God. These seven last plagues comprise the grand finale, a climax of God's wrath poured out on a sinful and degenerate world.

They recall a number of the plagues which God poured out on Egypt, virtually destroying the nation (Ex. 10:7). These end-time plagues or afflictions fall on those who refuse to acknowledge the government of God, and/or align themselves with the Antichrist and the False Prophet.

The events which accompany the vial or bowl judgments are:

**1. The First Vial:** The first angel pours out his vial of God's wrath on the earth. As a result a deadly pestilence strikes those who have accepted the mark of the beast (666). They accepted this mark so that they might live. Now they pay for it with terrible suffering.

It would appear that God is engaged in a type

# The End of this Age
# The Beginning of a New Era

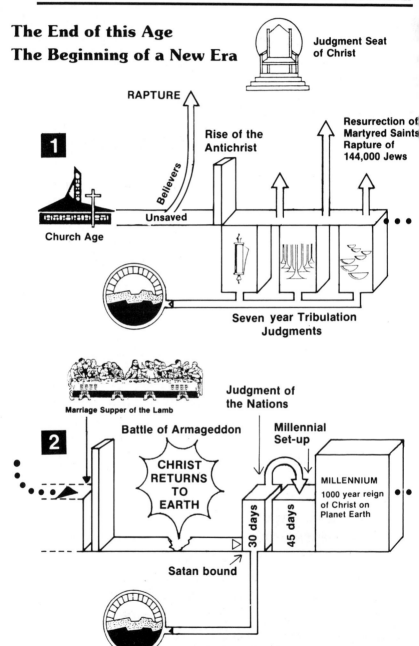

Judgment Seat
of Christ

**RAPTURE**

Rise of the
Antichrist

Resurrection of
Martyred Saints
Rapture of
144,000 Jews

**1**

Believers

Unsaved

Church Age

Seven year Tribulation
Judgments

Marriage Supper of the Lamb

Judgment of
the Nations

**Battle of Armageddon**

Millennial
Set-up

**2**

CHRIST
RETURNS
TO
EARTH

30 days

45 days

MILLENNIUM
1000 year reign
of Christ on
Planet Earth

Satan bound

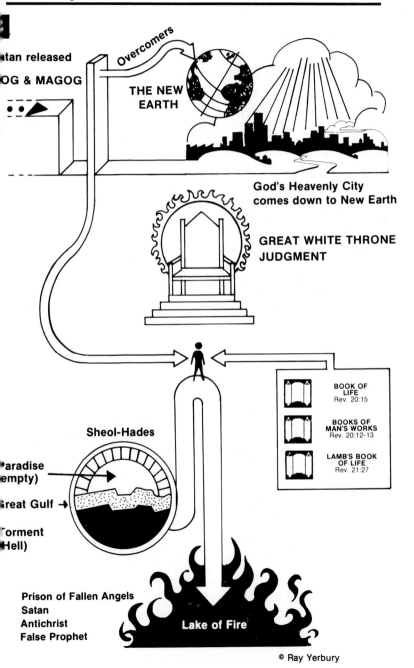

Satan released

GOG & MAGOG

Overcomers

**THE NEW EARTH**

**God's Heavenly City comes down to New Earth**

**GREAT WHITE THRONE JUDGMENT**

Sheol-Hades

Paradise (empty)

Great Gulf →

Torment (Hell)

BOOK OF LIFE
Rev. 20:15

BOOKS OF MAN'S WORKS
Rev. 20:12-13

LAMB'S BOOK OF LIFE
Rev. 21:27

**Prison of Fallen Angels
Satan
Antichrist
False Prophet**

**Lake of Fire**

© Ray Yerbury

of "germ warfare" upon the followers of the Antichrist and the False Prophet. This judgment compares with the sixth plague that fell upon the nation of Egypt in the days of Moses.

**2. The Second Vial:** The sea turns into blood and kills every living creature in it (v.3). The picture here is a catastrophe almost beyond human comprehension. The seas will wallow in blood. Under the second trumpet, one third of all the sea creatures died (Rev.8:9). Now the destruction is complete. The stench and disease that this will cause along the shores of all the seas of the earth (not only the Mediterranean Sea), will be unimaginable.

**3. The Third Vial:** When the angel poured his vial out upon the earth, all the rivers and springs of water became blood (vv.4-7). God's judgments, though fearsome, are said to be "true and righteous." This judgment would appear to be a duplicate to that on Egypt as recorded in Exodus 7:19-24.

Since Christians and God's faithful of the Old Testament - the prophets - had to shed their blood for what they believed, Christ now gives their murderers blood to drink. God's judgments are always true and just. This is the answer to the cry of the martyrs under the altar at the beginning of the Tribulation. Their prayer at that time was, *"How long, Sovereign Lord, holy and true, until you judge the inhabitants of the earth and avenge our blood ?"*

These verses also inform us that God has assigned special angels as controllers of the world's water supply. When we compare this with the four angels of Revelation chapter 7 who control the earth's winds, we realize that even during the hellish judgments of the Tribulation, this world is still in the control of Almighty God.

**4. The Fourth Vial:** The fourth angel poured his vial out upon the sun, resulting in an intensity of its rays directed upon the earth (vv.8-9). It scorches men with fire. Even though a third part of the sun was darkened under the fourth trumpet judgment (Rev.8:12), that which is left will be so powerful that it will "scorch people with fire."

What was the attitude of mankind to this judgment? Put simply, stubbornness. They still would not repent of their sins. One would think that this experience would drive people to their knees in repentance before the God of the creation. Instead they cursed God. Mankind's suffering will only harden their hearts. This illustrates how rebellious and hostile the human heart can be against their creator.

#### What will Finally Happen to these People?

The prophet Malachi puts it succinctly: "*Surely the day is coming; it will burn like a furnace. All the arrogant and every evildoer will be stubble, and that day that is coming will set them on fire, says the Lord Almighty. Not a root or a branch will be left in them. But for you who revere my name, the Sun of righteousness will rise with healing in its wings*" (Mal.4:1).

**5. The Fifth Vial:** When the fifth angel poured out his vial upon the earth, the Beast's kingdom was plunged into total darkness. Apparently from this statement we may conclude that this special judgment is directed on the headquarters of the Antichrist - the land of the ten nations of the revived Roman Empire will become dark. As a result of this darkness, men will gnaw their tongues in agony, and curse God because of the pains of their sores (v.10). Again we read these tragic words, "....*but they refused to repent of what they had done.*"

## Darkness Judgment Predicted by the Prophets

This judgment is a repetition of the ninth plague of Egypt (Ex.10:22), and was foreshadowed by a number of the Old Testament prophets.

"*Woe to you who long for the day of the Lord! Why do you long for the day of the Lord? That day will be darkness, not light*" (Amos 5:18).

"*That day will be a day of wrath, a day of distress and anguish, a day of trouble and ruin, a day of darkness and gloom, a day of clouds and blackness*" (Zeph.1:15).

"*Who can withstand His indignation? Who can endure his fierce anger? His wrath is poured out like fire; the rocks are shattered before him. The Lord is good, a refuge in time of trouble. He cares for those who trust in Him, but with an overwhelming flood He will make an end of Nineveh; he will pursue His foes into darkness*" (Nahum 1:6-8).

Christ also made His own prediction about the heavenly bodies during the Tribulation: "*But in those days following the distress, the sun will be darkened, and the moon will not give its light.*" (Mk.13:24).

**6. The Sixth Vial:** The sixth angel brings a two-part judgment to the land of Iraq.

**a)** This is a specific judgment on the Euphrates River which will dry up in preparation for the **"Battle of the Great Day of God Almighty"**, or what is incorrectly referred to as "The Battle of Armageddon." (See Chapter 16 for further detail)

**b)** The tremendous demon forces that go forth to bring the rebellious armies of the world to the Valley of Megiddo for the purpose of opposing the Lord.

The picture that is painted is that of the Lord, the God of the Universe, using psychological warfare upon His enemies. This is allowed in accordance with His Divine plan, the evil workings of the "the two Beasts" to so condition the minds of the leaders of the nations that they will make the decision to assemble themselves together as one unit, a mighty world army, ready to march on Israel from the East.

### The Euphrates River

The Euphrates River, situated in the modern land of Iraq, is first mentioned in the Bible associated with the Garden of Eden (Gen.2:14). It formed a natural barrier between the east and the west. It was the eastern border of the land that God gave to Abraham in the covenant of Genesis 15:18. It also served as the eastern border of the Old Roman Empire. Here the first godless city was built by Cain, and named after his son Enoch (Gen.4:17). It is also at this same locality that the last rebellious city (Babylon) will be constructed by the forces of the Antichrist (see Rev.18).

### Who are "the Kings of the East?"

The Bible does not specifically mention the nations by name, but we do know there will be some sort of a confederacy formed between a number of nations, for the word "kings" is plural. We are also told that they are from the east - that is, east of the land of Israel. As the time draws closer to the end of the Tribulation, the world will observe the drying up of the Euphrates River, and a massive army coming from the east will march towards Israel to assemble in the valley of Megiddo and on the plains of Jezreel.

*"Then they gathered the kings together to the place that in the Hebrew is called Armageddon"* (Rev. 16:16).

## Armageddon

The book of Revelation now introduces its readers to one of the more popular but least understood words in the Apocalypse. The word Armageddon was used quite frequently by the media reporters during the recent Middle East war. The World Book Dictionary describes the word Armageddon as "the place of a great and final conflict between the forces of good and evil at the end of the world."[1]   Sadly, it also suggests that a way of preventing Armageddon is the control or the ban on long-range missiles."

The word *Armageddon* is found only once in the Bible, here in Revelation 16:16. The word means or refers to the "hill of Megiddo." The place is located in the modern state of Israel, about 90 kilometres north of Jerusalem, and about 25 kilometres due east of the the commercial city of Hafia. N.P. Megiddo itself is a huge mound of civilizations, built upon one another. From the top of this hill there is commanding view of the long and fertile valley of Jezreel. It is reported that Napoleon Bonaparte on one occasion was heard to say that all the armies of the world could do battle in this ideal valley.

How right he was in that statement! Actually it has already served as a battle-ground of many major wars. It was adjacent to the neighbouring hill of Mount Tabor that Barak defeated the Canaanites (Judg.4:15); Gideon defeated the Midianites (Judg.7). Josiah met his death at Megiddo, located in the plains of Esdraelon, in the valley of Jezreel.

A careful investigation of the Scriptures will reveal that there will not be a single battle called "The Battle of Armageddon." Armageddon will merely be the assembling area for the immense armies of the world, particularly for the forces or "the kings" from the east. The actual war is correctly called, "The Battle on the Great Day of God Almighty (Rev.16:14). It will be fought farther south, in the "Valley of Jehoshaphat", which is considered by many scholars to be another name for the Kidron Valley, east of Jerusalem (Refer Joel 3:1-2, 9-14; Zech.14:1-15).

(For further details of this climactic battle, see chapter 16.)

In the Biblical account of this final war, we

note from chapter 16 that evil spirits controlling
"the Beast" and "False Prophet" go forth to deceive
the nations (v.13). They influence "*the kings of the
earth and of the whole world, to gather them for the
battle of the Great Day of God Almighty* " (v.14).

Contingents of armies from all nations will
converge on Israel to fight the returning Messiah.
However, just at the point when all seems lost for
Israel, Jesus Christ will appear with the armies
from Heaven. The confrontation between these
armies advancing on Jerusalem and other strategic
localities will result in "the Battle of the Great Day
of God Almighty."

The result of the battle will be inevitable. The
supernatural Christ will lead His army of resurrected
saints to total victory (Zech.14:1-15). The speed,
ferocity, and blood-shed of this war will make the
recent Middle East war, and any others for that
matter, pale into insignificance.

These harrowing events occur during the time
of the "wrath of God" as the Messiah puts down
all opposition to his rule. Christ must replace the
world's political, social, religious and economic
systems so that He can begin all things new (Isa.
2:2-4; 11:1-9). What was originally established in
the Garden of Eden prior to "the fall", will again be
re-established on this earth, without the influence
of Satan, and under the direct control and reign of
Jesus Christ. He is the King of kings, and Lord of
lords.

**7. The Seventh Vial:** When the seventh angel
poured out his vial into the air a voice will be heard

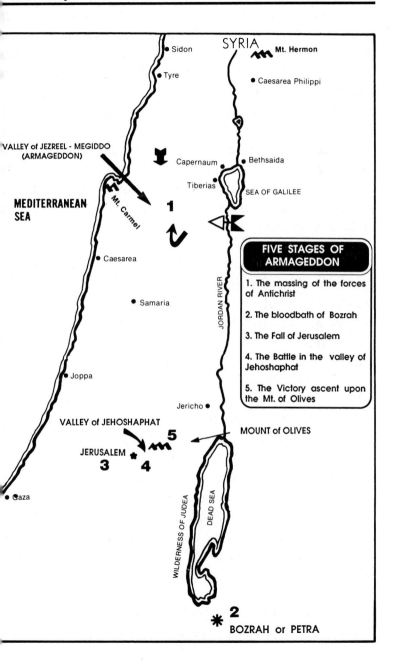

FIVE STAGES OF ARMAGEDDON

1. The massing of the forces of Antichrist

2. The bloodbath of Bozrah

3. The Fall of Jerusalem

4. The Battle in the valley of Jehoshaphat

5. The Victory ascent upon the Mt. of Olives

from the Temple of God. This will be the most awesome news the universe has ever heard. The voice proclaims a similar message to that heard on the cross: "It is done!" It signifies the consummation of the Tribulation, the end is near, the conclusion of the "day of wrath" upon ungodly men. "The time of Jacob's trouble" is over.

The final judgment of God is delivered by this seventh angel, and comes in the form of the world's greatest earthquake, causing widespread destruction and devastation. There is lightning and thunder as well as a great earthquake.

There have been many big earthquakes. In fact, the scientists tell us their numbers are increasing at an exponential rate. This particular one will be more intense than any previous quake. Maybe it  might measure 10 on the Richter scale?

As a result of this earthquake, "the great city" will split into three parts. This could be a reference to either Jerusalem or Babylon. In addition, many other cities will fall (v19). Islands and mountains of the world are also affected. The topography of the countries, particularly around the Mediterranean, will greatly alter in shape. The severity of God's judgment can be seen in the biggest hailstorm in all history. Great lumps of ice weighing 40 kilograms will fall from the sky and literally crush mankind.

Standing in the way of these remarkable changes is "Babylon the Great"- a symbol for all that is evil in the present world. The next chapter details how this Babylonish system is exterminated.

**Note:**
1. The World Book Dictionary. 1974. p115.

# Chapter 14

---

# The Fall of
# Babylon The Great

Babylon has played a significant role in Biblical history since the creation of the world. The Bible mentions Babylon 280 times, and many of those references give specific detail to the predominance of a future city that will rise from the sand dunes of the desert in modern Iraq.

The Old Testament prophets had much to say about Babylon:

*"Babylon, the jewel of kingdoms, the glory of the Babylonians' pride, will be overthrown by God like Sodom and Gomorrah"* (Isa.13:19).

Much of the present day confusion centers around the question: Was Babylon ever destroyed as the prophet Isaiah predicted? The simple, clear answer is NO. It was never suddenly overthrown like Sodom and Gomorrah. It was, however, conquered by the Medes and Persians and over the decades has fallen into decline and been covered by the sands of the desert. Much of the building material of ancient Babylon has been used in the construction of the nearby town of Al-Hilla, several kilometers away. Some materials were taken by Hitler for reconstruction in the Pergamon Museum located in Berlin, Germany. BUT, the city was not violently destroyed as predicted by Isaiah and John in Revelation 16:19; 18:10).

Isaiah had more to say about Babylon:
*"An oracle concerning Babylon that Isaiah son of Amoz saw......... wail, for the day of the Lord is near; it will come like destruction from the Almighty"* (Isa. 13:2).

The day of the Lord described by Isaiah in this passage directly refers to the time of the coming Tribulation period. Babylon's destruction will then take place, just before the Second Coming of Jesus Christ:

*"The Lord will have compassion on Jacob; once again He will choose Israel and will settle them in their own land. Aliens will join them and unite with the house of Jacob. Nations will take them and bring them to their own place. And the house of Israel will possess the nations as menservants and maidservants in the Lord's land. They will make captives of their captors and rule over their oppressors. On the day the Lord gives you relief from suffering and turmoil and cruel bondage, you will take up this taunt against the king of Babylon: How the oppressor has come to an end! How his fury has ended!.....All the lands are at rest and at peace; they break into singing"* (Isa. 14:1-4, 7).

When Babylon is ultimately destroyed just prior to Christ's coming, Israel will finally be at peace and will dwell in safety with their King, reigning from the Millennial Temple in Jerusalem.

## A.  Religious Babylon Destroyed

In the 17th chapter of Revelation, John records his vision of another hideous and distorted creature: "*Then the angel carried me away in the Spirit into a desert. There I saw a women sitting on a scarlet beast that was covered with blasphemous names and had seven heads and ten horns*" (Rev.17:3).

The women has a name on her forehead:
"*MYSTERY BABYLON THE GREAT
THE MOTHER OF PROSTITUTES
AND OF THE ABOMINATIONS OF
          THE EARTH*" (v.5).

She is pictured as being, "*drunk with the blood of the saints.*" In other words, she persecutes and martyrs the people of God (v.6).

The first six verses of Revelation chapter 17 reveal to us a most astounding and awful scene. They portray through symbols two great systems operating throughout the world, one religious and the other commercial and governmental.

Both chapters 17 and 18 portray the judgment of God upon this great madman - "the mother of harlots" and the "scarlet beast" she rides or controls.

It is clear that we are not dealing with a human being, for no one woman could commit adultery with the kings of the earth, nor could any one woman be "drunk with the blood of the saints, and the blood of those who bore testimony to Jesus." In Old Testament prophecy the image of a harlot is commonly used as a metaphor for a godless religious system of worship (Refer Isa.1:21; Ezek.16:15). Isaiah mocked Babylon by calling her a "virgin daughter" (Isa.47:1).

## Who is the Scarlet Beast?

Who is this strange "Scarlet Beast" with seven heads and ten horns, carrying the harlot woman? The interpretation given by the angel in verse 8 gives us the clue. This description is similar to the Beast of Revelation chapter 13, and doubtless represents what all beasts used symbolically represent - either a king or a kingdom that functions in total opposition to the Divine plan and will of Almighty God. So what we are talking about here is none other than the person of the Antichrist.

This Scarlet Beast and his ten horns [which represents ten kings or nations who will reign with him (Antichrist) during the Tribulation], all hate the woman (harlot - the evil apostate, satanic church), and will attack her and leave her naked and ravaged by fire (v.16).

## Who or What is the Harlot?

As we have already said, the term "harlot" is used symbolically by God to describe in vivid language any evil, apostate religious system opposed to the worship of the <u>one</u> and only true God - Jesus Christ. But why would God use the figure of a harlot to describe this system which will be in operation during the Tribulation period?

During Old Testament times Israel who was

described as the "Wife of Jehovah", often turned their backs on Jehovah to worship idols - the gods of the other nations. They simply became unfaithful to the one to whom Israel was married through the covenant given to Abraham. In other words, they committed spiritual adultery, and this is why the figure of a harlot is used (refer to the book of Hosea).

Any religious system that turns its back on the creator, the one who provides the very environment for worship, is an apostate or false religious system.

## What is this Religious System Called?

It is called MYSTERY BABYLON. Why? The word "mystery" is not used is this particular incident as an adjective to describe the noun Babylon. Rather the word itself is a noun used in joint association with Babylon. Put simply, we are not describing a place called Babylon located on the Euphrates River, but rather we have here a secret or mysterous use of the word Babylon.

It is mysterous because it is totally foreign to that which was ordained by God: that is, the TRUE church described as a mystery (Eph.5:32).

## Why is it Referred to as "Babylon?"

Babylon the city had its beginnings after the flood on the fertile plains of Shinar (Sumer), later known as Mesopotamia, and more recently as Iraq. Genesis chapter 10 tells us that Nimrod, a decendant of Ham, the unworthy son of Noah, built his kingdom at Babylon. Nimrod was not satisfied just with his earthly material exploits, but proceeded to establish his own brand of religious system by building the Tower of Babel (Gen.11). He tried to construct another way to God instead of using the sacrificial system God had commanded. Satan's church officially began at the Tower of Babel, with Nimrod as Satan's first full-time minister.

It was in the area of the city of Babylon that the first known lie was recorded (Gen.3:1); the first murder was committed (Gen.4:8); the first war was fought (Gen.14:14); and from Satan's headquarters sin spread its ugly tentacles throughout the world.

Representative of all false religions is the system that has become known as Babylon. The city of Babylon has declined through the ages, falling into the category of a ghost town, but never totally destroyed as was Sodom and Gomorrah. Although the city and the nation of Babylonia declined, its false, counterfeit  brand of religious worship continued to exert a powerful influence throughout the world.

Satan was alive and active.  He shifted his headquarters to Pergamum during the first century A.D. (Rev.2:13).   Today he continues to infiltrate the hearts and lives of people in all the cities and towns of the world.

It is this mystery Babylon that will revolt against God's eternal purposes during the Tribulation period.

## Is Mystery Babylon at work Today?

There is clear evidence that the world today is being conditioned to readily accept this end time counterfeit religion. The New Testament writers gave vivid details of its characteristics and her latter-day activities.

**1.** The apostle **Paul** said: *"But mark this: There will be terrible times in the last days. People will be lovers of themselves, lovers of money, boastful, proud, abusive, disobedient to their parents, ungrateful, unholy, without love, unforgiving, slanderous, without self-control, brutal, not lovers of the good, treacherous, rash, conceited, lovers of pleasure rather than lovers of God - having a form of godliness but denying its power..."* (2 Tim.3:1-4).

*" For the time will come when men will not put up with sound doctrine. Instead, to suit their own desires, they will gather around them a great number of teachers to say what their itching ears want to hear. They will turn their ears away from the truth and turn aside to myths "* (2 Tim.4:3-4).

**2.** The disciple **Peter** said: *"But there were also false prophets among the people, just as there will be false teachers among you. They will secretly introduce destructive heresies, even denying the sovereign Lord who bought them - bringing swift destruction on themselves "* (2 Pet.2:1).

**3. John** the beloved disciple and theologian had this to say: *" I know your deeds, that you are* *neither cold nor hot. I wish you were either one or the other! So, because you are lukewarm - neither hot nor cold - I am about to spit you out of my mouth. You say, I am rich, I have acquired wealth and do not need a thing. But you do not realise that you are wretched, pitiful, poor, blind, and naked"* (Rev.3:16).

This harlot church, the end-time satanic false religious system, will probably draw its membership from the apostate masses of Protestantism, Catholicism, Judaism, and a mixture of all the false cults and religions from around the world. Doubtless many of these people may have joined this false church as a reaction to the chaos in the world after the true church has been Raptured.

### The Future Activity of the Satanic Church

**1**. Her influence will be worldwide (v.1).
**2**. Her influence will reach to the highest levels of leadership  worldwide (v.2).
**3.** She is the force behind the throne, at least in the initial stages of the marriage. The beast will ultimately  wield the real power (v.3).
**4.** She will possess vast and unlimited wealth (v.4).
**5**. She will advertise her trade in order to trap new converts (v.5).
**6.** She will eliminate any who dare to question her false theology (v.6).  Only eternity will reveal how many people have been murdered in the name of religion.
**7.** The organizational headquarters for this false religious church could be the city of Rome (v.9). Rome sits upon seven mountains.

## What will be the Future of this False Church?

According to Revelation chapter 17 this false church, with its emphasis on organizational unity and oneness (the very theme of the New Age Movement) will lend all her evil strength and influence to elevate and exalt the Antichrist during the first half of the Tribulation (v.13). They both have a common purpose, and that is a hatred against the Lamb - Jesus Christ (v14). This association initially flourishes, but suddernly the marriage of convenience turns sour. John says, *"The beast and the ten horns you saw will hate the prostitute. They will bring her to ruin and leave her naked; they will eat her flesh and burn her with fire"* (v.16).

## Why would the Antichrist want to Destroy the Church?

A possible reason may stem from the fact that after the ecumenical church (harlot/woman) puts the Beast (Antichrist) in power, she then attempts to control him. History gives many examples of the Roman Catholic Church and other religious systems attempting to control kings and rulers. But the Antichrist won't be dictated to. He will turn on her with devastating results. He will destroy her buildings, burn her holy books and murder the priesthood.

The false and evil church will not be eliminated by the righteous judge or even by a holy angel. Ironically, it will be devastated and crushed by an evil despot - the Antichrist and his team of henchmen.

# B. Commercial Babylon Destroyed

In both chapter 17 and 18 two Babylons are presented. The Babylon we have just considered in chapter 17 is ecclesiastical or religious. We now consider the Babylon of chapter 18, which is commercial or economic, with a government flavour.

## Comparison of the Two Babylons

| CHAPTER 17 | CHAPTER 18 |
|---|---|
| 1.This Babylon is an ecclesiastical system. | 1.This is an economic and commercial system. |
| 2.It is very powerful. Attempts to control the affairs of mankind. | 2.Initially is controlled by the harlot. Finally wields the real power. |
| 3.Is ruthless in the execution of judgment to anyone who opposes its aims and ideology. | 3.It will appear to be the system that offers hope and prosperity for the business men of the world. |
| 4.This apostate church is hated by the kings of the earth. | 4.Commercial Babylon is loved by the kings of the earth. |
| 5. Mystery Babylon is destroyed in the midst of the Great Tribulation. | 5.Political Babylon is destroyed by the judgment of God at the 2nd coming. |

In chapter 18 the apostle John hears another shout: "*Fallen! Fallen is Babylon the Great! She has become the home for demons and a haunt for every evil spirit, a haunt for every unclean and detestable bird* " (v2).

The city called "Babylon" stands as the symbol for this anti-God materialistic system that has swayed and oppressed the human race. To the citizens of the world, however, the system does not appear evil at all. On the contrary, it seems to offer mankind what he has always sought. It appears to bring great economic prosperity to the nations of the world.

The majority of chapter 18 is taken up with this theme. "Babylon the Great" is seen as an economic market of great breadth and power. It is fabulously wealthy. The list of imports and exports that this power controls is impressive to say the least (Rev.18:11-15). The merchandise index listed in chapter 18 is similar to the one found in Ezekiel 27:12-24. There the Phoenician city of Tyre is the metaphor for a power that controls world trade.

## An Economic Superpower

Babylon, used in the sense of depicting the commercial and economic system of the world during the Tribulation period, makes businessmen rich and ushers in a period of general prosperity. John writes, "*The merchants of the earth will weep and mourn over her because no-one buys their cargoes any more*" (v.11). N.P. Then he continues listing the great array of precious desirable goods.

But finally a great cry goes forth: "....... *Woe! Woe, O great city, dressed in fine purple and scarlet, and glittering with gold, precious stones and pearls! In one hour such great wealth has been brought to ruin.......... They will throw dust on their heads, and with weeping and mourning cry out: Woe! Woe, O great city, where all who had ships on the sea became rich through her wealth! In one hour she had been brought to ruin*" (vv.16-19).

## Who will Judge Babylon?

God will be the final judge of this evil system. We read in the next chapter: ".....Salvation and glory and power belong to our God, for true and just are His judgments. He has condemned the great prostitute who corrupted the earth by her adulteries. He has avenged on her the blood of His servants" (Rev.19:2).

A strong and mighty angel now takes a great millstone and throws it into the sea (v.21). The throwing down of Babylon will be like that: it will be with great violence. No longer will there be heard the pleasant sounds of all types of musical instruments (v.22). Neither will the neon signs and bright city lights, indicative of an affluent economy, shine any more. All cause for celebration will have ceased.

## What was the Reason for this Destruction?

This evil worldly system destroyed God's messengers and so will be judged by God Himself.

## Will Babylon be Rebuilt?

The whole question as to whether Babylon will be rebuilt in the future has been subject to much debate among Biblical scholars for decades. Both sides have produced convincing arguments to support their point of view.

It is this writer's opinion that chapters 17 and 18 of Revelation refer to:

**1.** A Religious Babylon - the apostate church
**2.** A Commercial Babylon - the greed of the rich.
**3.** The rebuilt literal city of Babylon.

From the references in Holy Scripture, there seems to be reasonable evidence to support the fact that Babylon will be rebuilt during the time of the Tribulation, and doubtless will serve as the headquarters for the Antichrist. The following points support this conclusion:

**1.** Ancient Babylon was never suddenly destroyed, as prophesied by Isaiah 13:19.

**2.** Jeremiah the prophet describes a literal Babylon in a similar manner to that given by John in Revelation 18.

**3.** Isaiah refers to the destruction of Babylon during the "day of the Lord" (Isa. 13:9). This is an Old Testament reference to the Tribulation period.

**4.** For a literal Babylon to be destroyed during the Tribulation period, it must be rebuilt before or during that period.

**5.** According to Isaiah 14, Israel will be at rest after Babylon is destroyed. Certainly this has not been the case for Israel of recent times, with

Saddam Hussein from Iraq (ancient Babylonia) endeavouring to direct his fire-power towards Israel in an effort to exterminate God's chosen people.

**6.** Jeremiah predicts that Babylon will drink of the cup of the wrath of God last among all the kingdoms of the earth (Jer.51).

**7.** The description of Revelation chapter 18 is more than just a system. It is best understood when the destruction is considered in the light of a literal city.

### The Old Testament Foreshadows Her Destruction

On a night in 539 B.C. the Babylon of the Old Testament was captured by the Medes and Persians. Only a matter of hours before, Daniel the prophet had read the fearful words of God's judgment to a frightened Belshazzar, Nebuchadnezzar's grandson. Daniel said,"*God has numbered your days and brought your kingdom to an end. You have been weighed on the scales and found wanting. Your kingdom is divided and given to the Medes and Persians*" (Dan.5:26-28).

Some day, in the not too distant future, God himself will once again write those fearful words across the skies of Babylon. It seems that we are living in the shadow of those days.

# Chapter 15

# The Marriage Supper
# Of The Lamb

After John in a vision sees Babylon destroyed, he hears an angel announcing a royal victory celebration hosted by the Lamb.This glorious event is celebrated by using heaven's greatest praise word- *Alleluia* (Hallelujah) ! This "roar of a great multitude" will eclipse "the Hallelujah Chorus" from Handel's Messiah, which is considered to be the most sublime expression of praise in the field of music.

The word "Hallelujah" appears some 24 times in the Old Testament book of the Psalms. In the New Testament it is found only in Revelation: the Holy Spirit has reserved this ultimate expression of praise to chapter 19 of this book.

The heavenly chorus continues: "*Let us rejoice and be glad and give Him glory! For the wedding of the Lamb has come, and the bride has made herself ready.*" Concerning the bride or the wife of the Lamb, John continues to write, "*Fine linen, bright and clean was given her to wear, for the fine linen stands for the righteous acts of the saints.*" Then the angel said to me,"*Write; Blessed are those who are invited to the wedding supper of the Lamb..*" (vv.7-9).

## The Jewish Marriage Custom

Before we consider the important question of **when** and **where** will the marriage take place, let us first look at the terms "*Marriage*" and "*Wedding Supper*" as related to Jewish Marriage customs in Biblical times.

Jewish Marriage customs in Biblical times involved three major steps.

**1. The Betrothal**. This was the first step of establishing the fact of a Marriage covenant that bound the man and the woman together as husband and wife (Mal.2:14; Matt.1:18-19). There was no physical union between the man and the woman at this stage, even though they were considered husband and wife.. If it were found that the woman had been unfaithful, a divorce could be easily arranged. (Note Matt.1:19.)

**2. Fetching of the Bride.** The next step is the fetching of the bride or wife by the groom from her house to his father's house (Matt.25:1-8). This taking of the bride was usually carried out at night, approximately one year after the betrothal. The act signified the consummation of the marriage through physical union of the bride and groom on the first night at the groom's father's house.[1] Since that second step was the essence of the Marriage ceremony, it was regarded as the Wedding or Marriage (Matt. 22:2-13; 25:10).

It is this "fetching of the bride" step that corresponds to the expression **"Marriage of the Lamb"** as recorded in Revelation 19:7.

**3. The Wedding Feast.** The final step was the Wedding breakfast or Marriage supper, to which invited guests came to join in the celebrations with the Wedding party. Once the Marriage had been consummated by the bride and groom, the Wedding guests would partake of the food and wine over a period of seven days. Thus the Marriage supper would last for one week (Gen. 29:21-23, 27-28; Jud. 14:1-2, 10-12, 17).

It is this third stage which corresponds to the expression **"Wedding Supper of the Lamb"** as recorded in Revelation 19:9.

## How do the steps of Jewish Marriage Customs relate to the Marriage of Christ to the Church?

**1.** The betrothal of Christ to the true church is currently taking place during this church age. The means of the betrothal is a personal faith and trust in Jesus Christ as Saviour (2 Cor. 11:2).

**2.** At some future time, Christ will *fetch* His bride, the body of Christ - the true church - from this world and present her to His Father's house in Heaven. This event is referred to as the "Rapture of the Saints" (Jn. 14:2, 3; 1 Thess. 4:13-18). Thus the "Marriage of the Lamb" will be complete.

**3.** After the Rapture of the church, and at some point just before the return of Christ to this earth with His saints. the "Wedding Supper of the Lamb" will take place, with the invited guests assembled and waiting.

## Who are the "Invited Guests?"

Then the angel said to me, " *Write: Blessed are those who are invited to the Wedding supper of the Lamb* " (Rev.19:9).

The bride and the bridegroom are always automatic participants to any wedding. They do not have to be invited. In fact, there would be no wedding in the strict sense of the term if there was no bride and groom. So the bride and groom could not be the invited guests.

There are a number of other groups of "saints" redeemed from the earth in Heaven in addition to the church.

**1.** There are those who have been Raptured during the first half of the Tribulation period called "Tribulation saints" (Rev.7:14).

**2.** There are the 144,000 sealed Jewish witnesses (Rev.7:4-8; 14:1-3).

**3.** The two super witnesses to the Jewish people in Jerusalem (Rev.11:12).

**4.** The Old Testament saints ( Eph.4:7-10).

In the light of this revelation we conclude that the "invited guests" are all those in Heaven as listed from 1 to 4, plus the myriads of angels looking on.

## When and Where Will the Marriage/Wedding Supper Take Place?

There are three main schools of thought regarding this issue:

**a)** The Marriage will take place when the

church is Raptured at the Second Coming of Christ, and the Marriage Supper will take place on earth during the Millennium.

**b)** The Marriage will occur in Heaven when the church is Raptured, before the commencement of the Tribulation period, and the Marriage Supper will take place on earth during the Millennium.

**c)** The Marriage will occur in Heaven at the time of the Rapture, before the commencement of the Tribulation period, and the Wedding Supper will take place in Heaven just before the return of Jesus Christ to earth.

## Evidence to Strongly Suggest that both the Marriage and the Supper take place in Heaven

**1.** It was established custom in the Hebrew culture that the Wedding or Marriage did not take place at the home of the bride. The bridegroom fetches the bride, and the Marriage always takes place in the home of the bridegroom or his parents, where the bridal table and chamber are ready.

In harmony with this custom, Christ made it quite clear that after preparing accommodation for His bride in His Father's house in Heaven, He would return to receive His bride for Himself so that His bride could be where He is, that is, in the Father's house in Heaven (Jn.14:1-3). At no time did Christ indicate that He would come and join His bride on earth.

This established Marriage custom of **coming, fetching, and taking,** is consistant with the teaching of Christ's coming for His saints (Rapture), fetching them from out of this sinful world, and taking them back to His home to meet the Father of the bridegroom.

**2.** In Biblical times - and indeed, even today to a somewhat lesser extent - the Marriage was a joyous festive occasion. The fetching of the bride by the groom was characterized by excitement, dancing, and much joy and gladness (Jer.7:34; 16:9; 33:11).

When Christ comes for the church, as the apostle Paul indicates in 1 Thessalonians 4:17, the church will be "caught up" or "Raptured." The word "Rapture" comes from the Latin "*raptus* or "*rapere*", and it is found in the expression "caught up" or "seized" with great joy and estacy.

As a parallel to the joy and excitement that Christians will experience when Christ comes **for** His saints, and when He comes **with** His saints to reign for 1000 years, the mood of the people on earth will be opposite to the joyous, festive mood of the Marriage. The Marriage customs of Biblical times provided a festival atmosphere for the Wedding guests. The Second Coming will provide a radically different kind of supper - a funeral supper of dead flesh for the birds of the earth (Rev.19:17).

**3.** The Wedding Breakfast or Supper was never held at the home of the bride. Custom dictated that the feast was held at the home of the bridegroom or his parents (Matt.22:1-4).

In harmony with this ancient custom, the Marriage Supper of the Lamb should take place at Christ's Father's house in Heaven, not at His Bride's dwelling place on earth. This militates against an earthly Marriage Supper of the Lamb. Therefore the Marriage Supper must take place before the Millennial Reign of Christ on planet earth.

**4.** In Biblical times, it was customary for the Wedding Supper to last for one week of seven days. In relation to the Marriage Supper of the Lamb, the seven years of the 70th week of Daniel chapter 9 seems to correlate to that time period.

It is the conviction of the writer that the **Marriage or the Wedding of the Lamb** commences at the time of the Rapture, when the bride and the bridegroom are united in the Father's house. Furthermore, the **Marriage Supper** does not commence at the time of the Rapture, simply because all the invited guests have not assembled themselves ready for the victory feast.

The vast multitude of Tribulation saints (Rev.7:14) are not complete in number until the mid-point of the Tribulation. The 144,000 Jewish witnesses are called home only at the mid - point of the Tribulation. The witnesses in Jerusalem are commissioned to preach the gospel for 1260 days of the Tribulation - again, the mid-point of the Tribulation.

Furthermore, the activity of the judgments of God's wrath upon sinful mankind, the final eviction of Satan from heaven (Rev.12:9) and the Bema judgment of the redeemed (2 Cor. 5:10), would all impact to distract the attention from what will otherwise be a unique and joyous occasion.

It would appear that this great banquet will take place at some time during the latter half of the

Tribulation period, most likely just prior to the
return of the Lord Jesus Christ with all of the saints.

## An Interesting Conclusion

If the Marriage and the Wedding Supper of the
Lamb do not take place just prior to the Second
Coming of Jesus Christ, why are they included in
the chapter that focuses on the Battle of Armageddon
and the Second Coming activities?

There are two possible reasons:

**1.** The Holy Spirit wants to draw a contrast
between the great whore, with all her evil plans
of world domination and unity, and the perfect pure
union of the bride of Christ.

**2.** To draw a comparison between the blessing
of those called to the Marriage Supper of the Lamb,
and the judgment of the rebels at the Second
Coming of Christ.

Hallelujah! For our Lord God Almighty reigns.

**Notes:**

1. Lockyer, Herbert. *All The Parables Of The Bible,*
   p.239.

# Chapter 16

# The Victory
## of the
# Second Coming

The book of Revelation in chapter 19 describes one of the most important events of human history. It is the Second Coming of the Messiah or the Lord Jesus Christ in great power and victory.

In fact, this one relatively small chapter of twenty-one verses describes in summary four **(4)** significant events, all under the umbrella of the Second Coming:

**1.** The Victory Song of the Redeemed after the judgment of the great harlot.

**2.** The Marriage and Wedding Supper of the Lamb in Heaven.

**3.** The Second Coming of Jesus Christ to reinstate God's government on this earth and reward God's faithful people.

**4.** The Battle of Armageddon where Christ destroys the armies of the Antichrist, captures the Beast and False Prophet alive, and throws them into the "lake of fire."

All Biblical history points to this one event, summarized in this chapter, for it looks forward to the time when Christ will come to earth to set up His Kingdom. The Cross is paramount to our theology, for without the victory of the Cross salvation would be incomplete. But Christ did die on the Cross and rose victorous from the grave, and because of that fact we also will rise victorous, to reign with Him for all Eternity.

## The Fifth Horseman of the Apocalypse

We considered the four horsemen of the Apocalypse in chapter 5, of page 41. There we saw a horseman riding a white horse, and we concluded he was the Antichrist.

Now John sees heaven open and a rider decending on a white horse (v.11). The horse is white to represent purity and victory, for He will defeat all His enemies when He comes.

There is little doubt in the minds of Biblical scholars that this rider is none other than Jesus Christ. Why? Because He is called faithful and true. Faithful in all, and to all, that He has promised. He is also true in all his dealings with mankind, in stark contrast to the rider in Revelation chapter 6, the false messiah promising relief from oppression, but failing in his mission. Christ is the only one who can and will bring in everlasting peace on earth, something mankind is ever searching for but cannot find, because he has rejected the "Prince of Peace."

Man's appointed judiciary can only bring judgment upon a person on the visible evidence, using hard facts. Sometimes the process of the judicial system can lead to a bias in man's judgment. Not so with Christ. He will judge in righteousness and make righteous war. He will put all enemies to rest at His Second Coming.

## Operation Armageddon

There is a considerable amount of information disseminated throughout Scripture on the subject of the Second Coming of Jesus Christ. One of the great difficulties in the study of eschatology is placing these events in a correct chronological sequence, in order to clearly establish what will transpire in " the Battle of Armageddon."

It is important to realize that the Battle of Armageddon takes place at the time of Christ's Second Coming. It is not, as many believe, one single battle restricted to a particular locality in Israel. Furthermore, it will not be a campaign like the recent Middle East war. The Battle will finish virtually before it begins, because it will be a confrontation between the forces of the Antichrist and the Armies of Heaven.

Under the leadership of Jesus Christ as Captain of the Heavenly hosts, the armies of man will be defeated by " the brightness of His Coming." John says, "*Then I saw the beast and the kings of the earth and their armies gathered together to make war against the rider on the horse and His army. But the beast was captured, and with him the false prophet.............. The two of them were thrown alive into the fiery lake of burning sulphur. The rest of them were killed with the sword that came out of the mouth of the rider on the horse, and all the birds gorged themselves on their flesh."*

There are five **(5)** principal stages of **Operation Armageddon**, leading to the physical return of Jesus Christ. In summary they are as follows:
   **1.** The Massing of the Forces of Antichrist;
   **2.** The Bloodbath of Bozrah;
   **3.** The Fall of Jerusalem;
   **4.** The Battle in the Valley of Jehoshaphat; and
   **5.** The Victory Ascent upon the Mount of Olives

# 1. The Massing of the Forces of Antichrist

The Battle of Armageddon has been the magical catch-cry of journalists every time a major war has broken out. During the recent war between the multi-national forces and Iraq, led by Saddam Hussein, the question as to whether this was Armageddon or not was raised on numerous occasions. While the term has been commonly used, it is really a misnomer, for nowhere does it say in the Bible that a battle will take place at Armageddon.

Armageddon, meaning the "mount or hill of Megiddo" ( see Chapter 13 page 112) is located at the western end of the Valley of Jezreel. What Christians generally refer to as Armageddon is really the "Valley of Jezreel." Armageddon is only the small mountain or large hill at its western end.

There will be no fighting in Armageddon itself. The Valley of Jezreel, guarded by the mountain of Megiddo, will merely serve as the gathering ground for the armies of the Antichrist. It will probably play a similar role to that played by England during the closing stages of World War 11. The allied forces gathered their armies together in England, but this was not where the final battle took place. The final battle began on the beaches of Normandy, France, on "D" Day. Armageddon will also serve as a marshalling ground for the launching of troops and weapons to other localities in Israel.

The word of God says in Revelation 16:16:

### *"Then they gathered to the place that in Hebrew is called Armageddon."*

The actual battle that will be fought throughout the land of Palestine is better and correctly known as *"The Battle on the Great Day of God Almighty"* (Rev.16:12).

This gathering of the nations is seen as a gathering against God the Father and Jesus Christ His Son. It is a last ditch effort on the part of the Antichrist and the False Prophet to annihilate God's chosen people, the nation of Israel. In seeking to destroy the Jews, the world will invoke the wrath of God, and to fight God and His armies is to sign one's death warrant.  N.P. This is exactly what will happen. It will not be the Antichrist who sets up his kingdom, but it will be God who will reign from Zion, and Satan and Antichrist will not be able to prevent it.

The gathering of the armies of all the nations of the world into the Valley of Jezreel will be the first stage of Operation Armageddon.

## 2. The Bloodbath of Bozrah

*"Who is this coming from Edom, from Bozrah, with his garments stained crimson? Who is this, robed in splendour, striding forward in the greatness of his strength? It is I, speaking in righteousness, mighty to save. Why are your garments red, like those of one treading the winepress? I have trodden the winepress alone, from the nations no-one was with me. I trampled in my anger and trod them down in my wrath; their blood spattered my garments, and I stained all my clothing. For the day of vengeance was in my heart, and the year of my redemption has come. I looked, but there was no-one to help, I was appalled that no-one gave support; so my own arm worked salvation for me, and my own wrath sustained me. I trampled the nations in my anger; in my wrath I made them drunk and poured their blood on the ground"* (Isa.63: 1-6).

Bozrah was the capital of the ancient territory of Edom whose early king was Jobab (Gen.36:33). Because of the Edomites' attitude to the Jewish people, God judged them and they were totally overthrown, never to resettle again. This was predicted by the prophet Amos (1:12).

Today, Bozrah is usually identified with modern Buseirah, situated in a mountainous region close to the northern boundary of Petra, Jordan. It is only some 40 kms south east of the Dead Sea. This popular tourist destination is a labyrinth of caves and deep ravines, a natural hiding ground should someone want to escape detection.

## Why will Christ first go to Bozrah in Jordan?

In the Olivet Discourse that is recorded in Matthew's Gospel, our Lord told the disciples about many of the events that would take place towards the end of this age. He told about disturbed nations, of wars, of false prophets, of apostasy within the Christian church (Matt.24:4-14).

Our Lord also told those disciples about an Antichrist who would come and prevent the Jews from worshipping and sacrificing in the Temple. (v.15). But He also indicated that because of the oppression in Jerusalem in those days, many should leave and hide in the mountains: "*.... then let those who are in Judea flee to the mountains. Let no-one on the roof of his house go down to take anything out of his house, let no-one in the field go back to get his cloak. How dreadful it will be in those days for pregnant women and nursing mothers! Pray that your flight will not take place in winter or on the Sabbath* " (vv. 16-20).

This passage of Scripture clearly indicates that there will be a mass exodus of Jews from Jerusalem during the last half of the Tribulation period. Verse 15 tells us that "*the abomination that causes desolation* " is the event where the Antichrist enters the Temple in mid-Tribulation and calls a halt to Temple sacrifices.

We are also told the place to where the Jews will flee. Jerusalem was the principal city of Judea, the borders of which extended to the south and to the east. It was occupied principally by the tribe of Judah. If a person living in the area of Judea was told to flee to the mountains, he would not go towards Mount Hermon in the north, but rather would head south east across the Dead Sea and into the hills towards Petra, Jordan.

### Why Jordan?

During this horrific period of anti-semitism, with war raging throughout the Middle East, and the Antichrist hell-bent on destroying the Jewish population, most nations of the world will join or support one side or another. However, the prophet Daniel tells us that Jordan will remain neutral: "*At the time of the end the king of the South will engage the king of the North........... He (Antichrist) will invade many countries and sweep through them like a flood. He will also invade the beautiful Land. Many countries will fall, but Edom, Moab, and the leaders of Ammon will be delivered from his hand*" (Dan.11:40-41).

Many of the Jewish people will flee to Jordan and hide in the caves and hills to escape the wrath of the invading armies of the Antichrist. It will be here that God will provide a safe refuge for his people, and will fight off the advances of the Antichrist's forces, as revealed in Revelation chapter 12:13-16.

## 3.   The Fall of Jerusalem

In chapter 18 we read of the destruction of Babylon, the world capital of the Antichrist during the Tribulation period. At the time this occurs, which will be at the closure of the seven years of Tribulation, the Antichrist will have his forces assembled in the Valley of Jezreel. Instead of deploying his massive forces to the east, he is directed by Satan to move south towards Jerusalem. This is Satan's campaign, and Israel's destruction and annihilation is his ultimate goal.

Zechariah was an immigrant from Babylon, brought by his grandfather to Palestine when the Jewish exiles returned under Zerubbabel and Joshua the High Priest. He was called upon to prophesy at a young age around 520 B.C. It is Zechariah among all the prophets who gives the clearest picture of the capture of Jerusalem by the armies of the Antichrist.

"*This is the word of the Lord concerning Israel........ I am going to make Jerusalem a cup that sends all the surroundings peoples reeling. Judah will be besieged as well as Jerusalem. On that day, when all the nations of the earth are gathered against her, I will make Jerusalem an immovable rock for all the nations. All who try to move it will injure themselves*" (Zech.12:1-3).

Zechariah continues his prophecy directed against Jerusalem in chapter 14:

"*A day of the Lord is coming when your plunder will be divided among you. I will gather all the nations to Jerusalem to fight against it; the city will be captured, the houses ransacked, and the women raped. Half of the city will go into exile, but the rest of the people will be taken from the city*" (Zech14:1-2).

From the Valley of Jezreel the forces of Antichrist

will move south towards Jerusalem, either through the Jordan Valley, or the central highway through Nablus (Samaria), or down the coastal highway via Haifa and Tel Aviv. With such a large mass of troops it is more than likely that all three major highways will be used. The land of Israel will be overrun with military forces, the likes of which would be unimaginable in the minds of present- day leaders in Israel.

Jerusalem will fall into Gentile hands. Half will escape to Jordan (exile), while the remainder will be captured by the Antichrist's forces.

The capture by the forces of the Antichrist will come at great cost to the multi-national troops under the direction of Antichrist. God will energize the Jewish forces to withstand the attack, inflicting heavy casualities.

Zechariah gives a vivid description of God's intervention and fighting on the side of the Jews:

*"Then the Lord will go out and fight those nations, as he fights in the day of battle"* (14:3). *"On that day I will strike every horse with panic and its rider with madness, declares the Lord. I will keep a watchful eye over the house of Judah, but I will blind all the horses of the nations. Then the leaders of Judah will say in their hearts, the people of Jerusalem are strong, because the Lord Almighty is their God. On that day I will make the leaders of Judah like a fire-pot in a woodpile, like a flaming torch among sheaves. They will consume right and left all the surrounding peoples, but Jerusalem will remain intact in her place. The Lord will save the dwellings of Judah first, so that the honour of the house of*

*David and of Jerusalem's inhabitants may not be greater than that of Judah. On that day the Lord will shield those who live in Jerusalem so that the feeblest among them will be like David, and the house of David will be like God, like the angel of the Lord going before them. On that day I will set out to destroy all the nations that attack Jerusalem "* (12:4-9).

These verses clearly demonstrate God's providential dealing with the Jewish people during the final assult by the forces of the Antichrist on Jerusalem. This is just prior to the actual intervention by the personal return of Jesus Christ at which time "all Israel will be saved" (Rom.11:25).

We are also told that the leaders will be so energized that they appear to strike down the enemy as quickly as the torch begins to burn up dry wood. The feeble among the Jews take on the strength of David, and the Davids among them take on the strength of the Angel of the Lord.

Micah the prophet also supports the fact that the Jews will be given strength beyond measure during the last hours of *"the Battle on the Great Day of the Lord God Almighty."* In chapter 4:11 we see the nations of the world assembled against Jerusalem for the purpose of destroying it. But in the course of doing so these nations will become like sheaves on the threshing-floor (v.12), with the Jewish forces inflicting injury beyond measure.

The last hours of fighting are drawing to a close. There remains yet one final campaign for the Lord to fight. It will be the bloodest of all. The nations will then be silenced forever.

# 4. The Battle in the Valley of Jehoshaphat

The Antichrist and his now somewhat depleted forces will move on many fronts. He will come from the north - Armageddon, and from the south - Bozrah in Jordan. They will march towards and surround Jerusalem, not by any deliberate military strategy of their own doing, but simply because God will be drawing them into a pincer for judgment.

The prophet Joel provides a detailed picture of the future judgment of the nations in the Valley of Jehoshaphat, which is considered by many Biblical scholars to be another name for the Kidron Valley, east of Jerusalem. This is what Joel had to say: *"In those days and at that time, when I restore the fortunes of Judah and Jerusalem, I will gather all nations and bring them down to the Valley of Jehoshaphat. There I will enter into judgment against them concerning my inheritance, my people Israel, for they scattered my people among the nations and divided up my land. They cast lots for my people and traded boys for prostitutes; they sold girls for wine that they might drink "* (Joel 3:1-3).

The judgments of God continue:
*"Proclaim this among the nations: Prepare for war! Rouse the warriors! Let all the fighting men draw near and attack. Beat your ploughshares into swords and your pruning hooks into spears. Let the weakling say, I am strong! Come quickly, all you nations from every side, and assemble there. Bring down your warriors, O Lord "* (vv.9-11).

The nations that have gathered against the Jews will now find themselves being trodden in the winepress by the King of the Jews. It is of this treading in the Valley of Jehoshaphat that Revelation 14:19-20 speaks:

*"The angel swung his sickel on the earth, gathered its grapes and threw them into the great winepress of God's wrath. They were trampled in the winepress outside the city, and blood flowed out of the press, rising as high as the horse's' bridles for a distance of 1600 stadia"* (300 kms.).

After the Lord judges and destroys all the enemies of the Jewish people, great blessings are promised for God's people. This will happen at Christ's Second Coming.

*"The Lord will roar from Zion and thunder from Jerusalem; the earth and the sky will tremble. But the Lord will be a refuge for his people, a stronghold for the people of Israel. Then you will know that I, the Lord your God dwell in Zion, my holy hill. Jerusalem will be holy; never again will foreigners invade her. In that day the mountains will drip with new wine, and the hills will flow with milk; all the ravines of Judah will run with water. A fountain will flow out of the Lord's house and will water the valley of acacias"* (Joel 3:16-18).

The fighting is now over. All of God's enemies have been defeated. The Antichrist and the False Prophet have been thrown into "the Lake of Fire." Satan is about to be bound by an angel for a thousand years. There remains one final event in the campaign of "the Great Day of the Lord God Almighty."

## 5. The Victory Descent upon the Mount of Olives

The ultimate event in all of man's history is graphically described in the great apocalyptic book of the Old Testament- Zechariah:

"............ *Then the Lord will go out and fight in the day of battle. On that day his feet will stand on the Mount of Olives, east of Jerusalem, and the Mount of Olives will be split in two from east to west, forming a great valley, with half of the mountains moving north and half moving south............ Then the Lord my God will come, and all the holy ones with him* " (Zech. 14:3-5).

The physical, visible return of Jesus Christ will be accompanied by many great cosmic disturbances as told by the prophet Joel:

" *Multitudes, multitudes in the valley of decision! For the day of the Lord is near in the valley of decision. The sun and moon will be darkened, and the stars no longer shine*" (Joel 3:14-15).

Along with the victory descent upon the Mount of Olives, a number of catalysmic events will occur on earth as a finale to the Great Tribulation:

"*On that day there will be no light, no cold or frost. It will be a unique day, without daytime or night-time, a day known to the Lord. When evening comes, there will be light. On that day living water will flow out of Jerusalem, half to the eastern sea (Dead Sea), and half to the western sea (Mediterranean Sea), in summer and in winter* " ( Zech. 14:6-8).

The visible return of Jesus Christ from Heaven to planet earth will not only result in the city of

Jerusalem splitting into three divisions (Rev. 16:19), but the Mount of Olives will also split into two parts from east to west, resulting in the formation of great valleys and relocated mountains. Apparently the Temple Mount where Jesus Christ will reign during the Millennium will be the highest point in the Holy City:

"......... *But Jerusalem will be raised up and remain in its place......... It will be inhabited; never again will it be destroyed. Jerusalem will be secure*" (Zech. 14:10-11).

"........ *in the last days the mountain of the Lord's Temple will be established as chief among the mountains; it will be raised above the hills, and all nations will stream to it......*" (Isa. 2:2).

Zechariah, under the leading of the Holy Spirit, now turns back the clock a few hours to give a brief description of the ferocity of the battle for Jerusalem.. The description of this attack in verse 12 strongly suggests radiation poison which points to the limited use of nuclear weapons:

"*This is the plague with which the Lord will strike all the nations that fought against Jerusalem. Their flesh will rot while they are standing on their feet, their eyes will rot in their sockets, and their tongues will rot in their mouths. On that day men will be stricken by the Lord with great panic. Each man will seize the hand of another, and they will attack each other.......... A similar plague will strike the horses and mules, the camels and donkeys, and all the animals in those camps*" (Zech. 14:12-13;15).

# THE SECOND COMING OF CHRIST

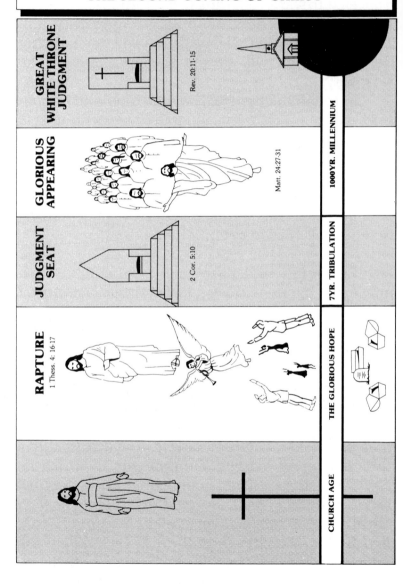

| CHURCH AGE | THE GLORIOUS HOPE | 7YR. TRIBULATION | 1000YR. MILLENNIUM | |
| --- | --- | --- | --- | --- |
| | RAPTURE | JUDGMENT SEAT | GLORIOUS APPEARING | GREAT WHITE THRONE JUDGMENT |
| | 1 Thess. 4: 16:17 | 2 Cor. 5:10 | Matt. 24:27-31 | Rev. 20:11-15 |

# Chapter 17

# Preparation for the Kingdom

The 20th chapter of Revelation sketches a very brief outline of God's plan for human beings. Again as we saw in the previous chapter, we are permitted to know the way and direction, however, as to the fine details, we will have to wait to experience that joy, which will be beyond measure. It is more important that we know for certain that we will be an integral part of God's plans during His earthly reign.

Six **(6)** major events transpire in this chapter. Three take place almost immediately on the return of Jesus Christ. The fourth, for which we are given no details in Revelation, transpires over a thousand year period. The fifth and sixth events occur at the conclusion of the Kingdom Period.

The six events are:
1. **The Removal of the Source of all Evil;**
2. **The First Resurrection;**
3. **The Judgment of the Nations;**
4. **The Millennial Reign of Jesus Christ;**
5. **The Spiritual Battle of Gog and Magog;**
6. **The Great White Throne Judgment.**

# 1. The Removal of the Source of all Evil

The event that clearly foretells the mid-point of the Tribulation will be that time of the takeover by the Antichrist of the rebuilt Jewish Temple. It is in this Holy Place that he will declare himself to be Almighty God. The Antichrist will also instruct the False Prophet to set up his image in the Temple, thus fulfilling the prophecy as recorded in the book of Daniel chapter 9:27:

*"He will confirm a covenant with many for one seven, but in the middle of that seven, he will put an end to sacrifice and offering. And the one who causes desolation will place abomination on the wing of the temple, until the end is decreed is poured out on him."*

Now we know that the Tribulation Period is to last exactly **7 years**, which is also equivalent to **2520 days** (the prophetic year = 360 days). Half of 2520 days is **1260 days**. But Daniel mentions two other time periods in relation to the "*abomination that causes desolation.*"

*"From the time that the daily sacrifice is abolished and the abomination that causes desolation is set up, there will be **1290 days**. Blessed is the one who waits for and reaches the end of the **1335 days**"* (Dan. 12:11-12).

## What does this extra time period represent?

The obvious question we ask is, "What happens during the additional **75 days**?"

There are actually two time periods mentioned

totalling  __75 days__. 1290-1260 days.= **30 days**.
1335-1290 days.= **45 days.**

a) __The extra 30 days.__    It is most probable that
this period of 30 days will be the time occupied to
accomplish:

i.    **The Binding of Satan;**
ii.   **The Resurrection of the Martyred Saints;**
iii.  **The Judgment of the Nations**

John sees in a vision an (ordinary) angel,
"....*come down out of Heaven having the key to the
abyss and holding in his hand a great chain. He
seized the dragon, that ancient serpent, who is the
devil, or Satan, and bound him for a thousand years.
He threw him into the abyss, and locked and sealed
it over him, to keep him from deceiving the nations
any more until the thousand years were ended.........*"
(Rev.20:1-3).

It is significant that at this point in God's plan
Satan is a defeated foe, powerless to resist his
binding in chains. The binder is not an archangel,
but simply a member of the ordinary rank of angels.
He binds this once anointed cherub and literally
throws him into the abyss, which is more than likely
the great gulf of Sheol or Hades that separates the
place of comfort from the place of torment.

Satan is bound in chains with the promise that
he will be released for a short period after the
thousand years are completed. At this point the
Antichrist and the False Prophet are already
residing in the fiery Lake of Fire. They were the first

people to sample God's garbage disposal furnace. Satan will join them one thousand years later.

**b). <u>The Additional 45 days</u>.** The language of Daniel 12:11-12 suggests that the 30 days will be filled with the activity of judgment, while on the other hand the additional 45 days would indicate a period of joy and blessing. This period will more than likely be taken up by our Lord allocating responsibilities for the saints during the Millennial Reign of Christ.

Whatever the exact nature and sequence of events that might take place during the time Jesus Christ is first upon this earth, one thing is certain: it will be a period of great activity and excitement for the child of God, but a time of intense anxiety for all who have rejected Christ.

## 2.   The First Resurrection

The First Resurrection is an event for believers only. It commenced with Jesus Christ, the first-fruits of those who had died in Christ (1 Cor. 15:20). It includes all those of the Church Age who have made a confession of faith in Christ, so when they die they go immediately to heaven to be with Jesus.

"........ *And I saw the souls of those who had been beheaded because of their testimony for Jesus and because of the word of God.......... They came to life and reigned with Christ for a thousand years...... This is the First Resurrection*" (Rev.20:4-5).

The souls referred to in this passage are all those who did not take the Mark of the Beast, but were martyred for their belief in Christ.

The resurrection of these martyred saints completes the first resurrection. It is separated from the completion of the second resurrection by a thousand years. The second resurrection is a resurrection to eternal damnation. This will climax in the event known as "The Great White Throne Judgment."

## 3.   The Judgment of the Nations

The word translated "nations" also means Gentiles. So this is a judgment of the Gentile people alive at the Second Coming of Jesus Christ. Although numerous Gentiles will be killed during "Operation Armageddon", many will still be alive to face the Judgment of the Nations, or what is also called "The Sheep and Goat Judgment."

The nature of this judgment is not a national one as the word "nation" suggests, but rather it is an individual one - Gentiles from all the nations.

Matthew's gospel provides a graphic picture of the mechanism of this judgment:

" *When the Son of Man comes in His glory, and all the angels with Him, He will sit on His throne in Heavenly glory. All the nations will be gathered before Him, and He will separate the people one from another as a shepherd separates the sheep from the goats. He will put the  sheep on his right side and the goats on his left* " (Matt 25:31-33).

### What is the basis of this judgment?

Each Gentile living at that time will be judged on the basis of his attitude and treatment of the Jews during the Great Tribulation. Furthermore, the people will also be judged on the basis of their attitude of heart towards Jesus Christ. Any who have taken the "Mark of the Beast" will be banished into everlasting punishment. These people will be the **"goats."** Those who have made a decision to follow Christ, or those who have not accepted the "Mark of the Beast", or who are undecided regarding their relationship to Jesus Christ, will be called blessed, and thus will enter the Millennial Kingdom in their fleshly bodies to live on the earth for a thousand years. These people will be called **"sheep."**

### What will be the Result of this Judgment?

The judge is Jesus Christ (Matt.25:31). He will be assisted by others seated on thrones, "*who have been given authority to judge* "(Rev.20:4). Each Gentile living will stand before the judgment throne. "The sheep" - those who are called blessed will enter the Millennial Kingdom and gain Eternal life. "The goats"- those who are called cursed - will enter into the eternal fire prepared for the devil and his angels ( Matt.25: 34-46).

## 4.  The Millennial Reign of Jesus Christ

This one thousand (1000) year period is often

referred to as "the Millennium." The word *Millennium* does not occur in the Bible as such. It comes from the Latin words *mille* and *ennium* meaning "one thousand" and " years."

The one thousand years' reign of Christ is mentioned five times, and only in chapter 20 of the Book of Revelation.

Premillennialists have often been criticized for basing their belief in a literal Millennium entirely on one chapter in a book that is noted for its frequent use of symbols. However, that is hardly a valid criticism, as we shall clearly demonstrate in the next chapter.

The Millennial Reign of Jesus Christ will commence with the physical, visible and literal presence of Christ in Jerusalem, Israel. The dwelling place of Jesus Christ - the Millennial Temple will be  considered in chapter 18.

## 5. The Spiritual Battle of Gog and Magog

This battle will occur after the Millennium. We will discuss this battle in chapter 20.

## 6. The Great White Throne Judgment

This will be the last and final judgment ever to take place for mankind. It is a judgment to eternal death in the "Lake of Fire." (An understanding of the process of this judgment and the various "books" that are opened to present the evidence before the accused will be detailed in chapter 20 under the heading, "The Clean-up Before Eternity.")

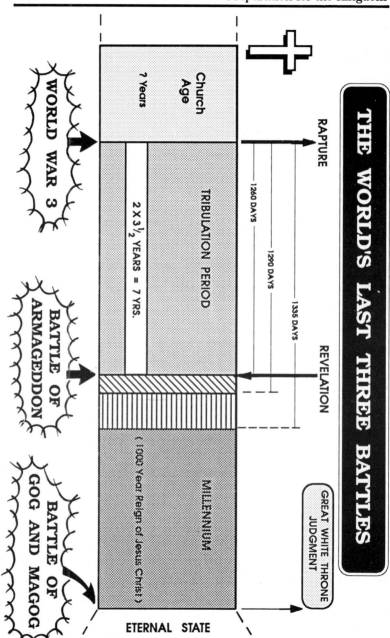

THE WORLD'S LAST THREE BATTLES

WORLD WAR 3

BATTLE OF ARMAGEDDON

BATTLE OF GOG AND MAGOG

Church Age

7 Years

TRIBULATION PERIOD

2 X 3½ YEARS = 7 YRS.

RAPTURE

1260 DAYS
1290 DAYS
1335 DAYS

REVELATION

MILLENNIUM

( 1000 Year Reign of Jesus Christ )

GREAT WHITE THRONE JUDGMENT

ETERNAL STATE

# Chapter 18

# The Coming New World Order- "The Millennium"

Ever since time began men has sought to build empires and become masters of the universe. Today's generation is no different in their quest for a utopian world, guided by a central authority and under the leadership of a popular Messiah. But to the majority of people, it does not take a university degree to realize that the world is having a giant hemorrhage.

The great Jewish/American physicist, Albert Einstein once said that mankind's desire for peace can be realized only by the creation of a world government.

Two years after the end of World War 11, British statesman Sir Winston Churchill declared, "Unless some effective world supergovernment can be set up and brought quickly into action, the prospects for peace and human progress are dark and doubtful."[1]

And so the world continues to cry out: What is the solution to the inflation problem, unemployment, crime waves, drug addiction, pollution, sexual immorality, armament build-up? Who is to blame for the existing conditions? It's popular to blame the politicians: after all, it's their job to solve the woes of society, but do they really care?

We see considerable unrest among the youth of our nations. They believe that the national leaders are too old and incompetent. The more mature leaders are blaming the education system for a restless youth, and so the blame ebbs to and fro across the sea of indecision, and no-one is really prepared to take the scalpel and to operate on the real cause of the cancer in our society - and that is SIN.

Many groups are emerging offering hope in a world gone mad. The New Age Movement, with its roots firmly planted in Eastern Hindu mysticism, promotes "mind sciences" and the concept of the "Age of Aquarius" or "A New World Order" as the only way of salvation for the world. They say the New Age Christ or "The Lord Maitreya" will soon appear to lead the world into the 21st century.

### What is God's Purpose for the World?

Isaiah the prophet from whom Jesus loved to quote had this to say about the purpose of this world: *"God formed the earth and made it; He fashioned and founded it; He did not create it to be empty, but formed it to be inhabited"* (Isa. 45:18).

This is very comforting - the earth is to be inhabited and not to become a desert void as pictured by the scaremongers of space fiction.

Again Isaiah declares:

*"The earth shall be full of the knowledge of the Lord, as the waters cover the sea"* (Isa. 11:9).

"*When God's judgments come upon the earth the people of the world will learn righteousness*" (Isa.26:9).

Now the idea of the "knowledge of the Lord and righteousness" doesn't rate too high among the people of the world today; but for all their contempt, the world must admit that ignorance of God and unrighteousness hasn't led us to any great heights on the moral and spiritual scale.

## A New World Order

During the past year we saw as never before rapid changes in world conditions. Governments rose and fell almost overnight. Wars and uprisings, deploying high technology were won or lost within weeks or even days. The catch-cry of "A New World Order" is heard every day by our national leaders. But it is a New World Order on man's terms and by man's actions. What most politicans and people in general forget, or rather do not want to believe, is that there is a New World Order coming, but it will be God who will usher it in.

The Bible declares:   "*The God of heaven will set up a kingdom that will never be destroyed, nor will it be left to another people. It will crush all those kingdoms and bring them to an end, but it will itself endure for ever*" (Dan.2:44).

"*The kingdom of this world will become the kingdom of our Lord and of His Christ and He will reign for ever and ever* " (Rev.11:15).

## When will this Utopian World come into Being?

Today we live in the shadow of the imminency of Christ's return for His church, the event known as the Rapture. After the Rapture there comes the Tribulation Judgments on earth, the Bema Judgment in Heaven, the Marriage Supper of the Lamb, followed by the Second Coming of Jesus Christ to earth.

The New World Order will commence when Jesus Christ sets up His throne in the New Jerusalem on earth to reign for 1000 years.

*".... The Lord God will give Him the throne of his father David, and He will reign over the house of Jacob for ever; His kingdom will never end"* (Lk. 1:32).

## Who will Live in the Millennial Kingdom?

In Jude verse 14, we have recorded prophey's first word from man:

*"Enoch, the seventh from Adam, prophesied about these men: See, the Lord is coming with thousands upon thousands of His Holy Ones."*

**Who are these Holy Ones?** If we can identify them, we will know who will reign and live with Christ in a new utopian society.

**1. Angels:** *"For the Son of Man is going to come in His father's glory with His angels, and then He will reward each person according to what he has done"* (Matt. 16:27).

*"...... You shall see Heaven open, and the angels of God ascending and decending on the Son of Man"* (John 1:51).

**2. All Believers of the Church Age:** All truly born-again believers who die prior to the Rapture. {Note: at death they go directly to heaven but remain in a "soulish state" (Phil. 1:21).} They will receive their glorified bodies first in accordance with 1 Thessalonians 4:16. Then we who are alive will be Raptured and immediately receive our glorified body (1 Cor. 15:53).

" *Look , He is coming with the clouds, and every eye will see Him, and all the people of the earth will mourn because of Him. So shall it be* " (Rev. 1:7).

## What are the Clouds?

They represent all the glorified believers coming with Christ from Heaven. They are clothed in. "*fine linen, bright and clean, which speaks of the righteousness of the saints*" (Rev. 19:8).

**3. The Tribulation Saints.** During the first three and one half of the Tribulation, there will be a great soul harvest won to the Lord as a result of the powerful witness of the 144,000 Jewish witnesses. Many will be put to death for their faith in Jesus Christ, as revealed in Revelation 7:13-17.

**4. The Sealed Jews.** The 144,000 Jewish witnesses of Revelation chapter 7 are the same group as seen in chapter 14. They now stand on Heavenly Mount Zion. How did they get there? They were raptured at the mid-point of the Tribulation.

**5. The Old Testament Saints.** Daniel in chapter 12 reveals that immediately after the description of the Great Tribulation in chapter 11, deliverance is now promised to Israel at the close of the Tribulation. They represent the invited guests to the Marriage Supper, which will take place just prior to the glorious appearing of Jesus Christ.

## Everlasting Peace will Come

When Jesus Christ returns to earth, He will establish a government that will have a platform of basically two policies - everlasting peace and blessing. But this will not be achieved in all nations immediately. This new society of peace and happiness won't be built in a day, with so many wrong ideas to unlearn and overcome. Nations will need to learn the Biblical way of holiness and happiness.

## Who will Administer the New Education Program?

The Jewish nation, under the direction of their now accepted Messiah will give the lead to the world in international affairs. However, it will be Christ and the resurrected (glorified) saints who will set about to teach the world the way of peace. Two great commandments will be the foundation for peace and happiness:

*"...... You shall love the Lord your God with all your heart and with all your soul and with all your mind"* and *"You shall love you neighbour as yourself"* (Matt. 22:37,39).

The prophet Isaiah describes this new kind of education:

*" Many people will say, come and let us go up to the*

*mountain of the Lord, to the house of the God of Jacob. He will teach us His ways, so that we may walk in His paths. The law will go out from Zion, and the word of the Lord from Jerusalem. He will judge between the nations and will settle disputes for many peoples. They will beat their swords into ploughshares and their spears into pruning hooks. Nation will not take up sword against nation, nor will they train for war any more"* (Isa.2:3-4).

Depicting this verse, outside the United Nations building in New York City is a striking bronze statue of a man beating a sword into a plow blade. The statue was a gift from the government of the Soviet Union to the United Nations. Fulfillment of this elusive ideal will, however, come to fruition during Christ's Reign as King of the whole earth.

## What will conditions be like on Earth during the Millennium?

**1. Israel will be Established in a "Garden of Eden."** The unconditional covenant established by God with Abraham will be finally and fully implemented:

*"I will make you into a great nation...... all people on earth will be blessed through you"* (Gen.12:2-3).

*"All the land that you see I will give to you and your offspring for ever......"* (Gen.13:15).

*"On that day the Lord made a covenant with Abram.... To your decendants I give this land from the river of Egypt to the great river, the Euphrates......"* (Gen.15:18).

*" I will establish my covenant with him as an*

*everlasting covenant for his decendants after him...
.....my covenant I will establish with Isaac "*
(Gen.17:19-21).

The Lord said to Jacob in a dream, " *I am the God of
your father Abraham and the God of Isaac. I will give
you and your decendants the land on which you are
lying. Your decendants will be like the dust of the
earth........ All people on earth will be blessed through
you and your offspring*" (Gen.28:13-14).

The fact of the covenant gives proof that the
Jews by which we mean the whole of the Israelite
nation, are to be given a vast parcel of land. The
area originally planned by God for His people has
never been completly occupied, but will be during
the Millennium, as shown on the map on page xii.

**What will happen to Eretz Israel?** ( Land of Israel)

**a) Abundant Water Supply.** "*In that day the
mountains will drip new wine, and the hills will flow
with milk; all the ravines of Judah will run with
water. A fountain will flow out of the Lord's house
and will water the valley of acacias*" (Joel 3:18).

**b) Bumper Crop Harvest.** "*The threshing-floors
will be filled with grain, the vats will overflow with
new wine and oil...... You will have plenty to eat, until
you are full* " (Joel 2:24,26).

**c) No more Famine in the Land.** "*I will bless them
and the places surrounding my hill. I will send down
showers in season; there will be showers of blessing.
The trees of the field will yield their fruit and the
ground will yield its crops*" (Ezek.34:26-27).

**d) A Surplus of Food and Wine for Export.** *"The days are coming declares the Lord when the reaper will be overtaken by the ploughman and the planter by the one treading grapes. New wine will drip from the mountains and flow from all my hills.... They will plant vineyards and drink their wine, they will make gardens and eat their fruit"* (Amos 9:13-14).

**e) Perfect Weather Conditions.** *"....I will send down showers in season......"* (Ezek. 34:26). *".. He sends you abundant showers both autumn and spring rains as before"* (Joel 2:23).

**f) Security of Tenure.** *"In that day the Lord will reach out His hand a second time to reclaim the remnant that is left of His people....."* (Isa.11:11).

*"The days are coming, declares the Lord.......I will bring back my exiled people Israel; they will rebuild the ruined cities and live in them. They will plant vineyards and drink their wine; they will make gardens and eat their fruit. I will plant Israel in their own land, never again to be uprooted from the land I have given them"* (Amos 9:13-15).

**g) A Perfect Enviroment.** *"No-one living in Zion will say I am ill, and the sins of those who dwell there will be forgiven"* (Isa.33:24).

*"....the eyes of the blind will be opened, the ears of the deaf unstopped, the lame will leap like a deer, and the tongue of the dumb will shout for joy. The water will gush forth in the wilderness and streams in the desert. The burning sand will become a pool, the thirsty ground bubbling springs. In the haunts*

*where jackals once lay, grass and reeds and papyrus will grow* " (Isa.35:5-7).

Isaiah chapter 65:17-25 gives the best picture of the environment and what living conditions will be like during the Millennial Reign of Jesus Christ on this earth:

*"I will rejoice over Jerusalem and take delight in my people, the sound of weeping and crying will be heard in it no more. Never again will there be in it an infant that lives but a few days or an old man who does not live out his years. He who dies at a hundred will be thought a mere youth; he who fails to reach a hundred will be considered accursed. They will build houses and dwell in them, they will plant vineyards and eat their fruit...... For as the days of a tree, so will be the days of my people...... They will not toil in vain or bear children doomed to misfortune; for they will be a people blessed by the Lord........ The wolf and the lamb will feed together, and the lion will eat straw like the ox, but dust will be the serpent's food. They will neither harm nor destroy in all my holy mountain says the Lord."*

**h)  No More Evil.** *"He will judge between many peoples and will settle disputes for strong nations far and wide. They will beat their swords into ploughshares and their spears into pruning hooks. Nation will not take up sword against nation, nor will they train for war any more"* (Micah 4:3).

*"...... Your throne, O God, will last for ever and ever, and righteousness will be the sceptre of your kingdom* " (Heb.1:8).

## 2. The Whole World will Enjoy the Blessings Promised to Israel

**a) One King:** (Jesus Christ) "The Lord will be King over the whole earth" (Zech. 14:9).

**b) A New Administration:** Directed by the glorified saints. *"The armies of heaven followed riding white horses"* (Rev19:13). *"They reigned with Christ for a thousand years"* (Rev.20:4).

**c) A Universal Religion of Truth:** " ... My name will be great among the nations" (Mal.1:11).
*"Then the survivors from all the nations.... will go up year after year to worship the King..."* (Zech.14:16).

**d) A United World:** " *All kings will bow down to him and all nations will serve him* " (Psalm 72:11).

**e) Total Disarmament and Abolition of War:** " *He will judge between the nations and will settle disputes for many people. ..... Nation will not take up sword against nation, nor will they train for war any more* " (Isa.2:4).

**f) A New Economic System:** *"Merchandise....her profit and earning will be set apart for the Lord; they will not be stored up or hoarded. Her profits will go to those who live before the Lord, for abundant food and fine clothes* " (Isa.23:18).

**g) International Peace and Goodwill:** " *...... Of the increase of his government and peace there shall be no end. He shall reign on David's throne .......with justice and righteousnees from that time on and forever'* " (Isa.9:7).

## h) Equitable Distribution of Wealth and Resources

*"They will build houses and dwell in them, they will*

*plant vineyards and eat their fruit. No longer will they build houses and others live in them, or plant and others eat* " (Isa. 65:21-22).

**i) Firm but Fair Government Control:** "*He will defend the afflicted among the people and save the children of the needy. He will rule from sea to sea, and from the river to the ends of the earth* " (Psalm 72:4.8).

**j) Vast Increase of the Earth's Productivity:** "*The days are coming, declares the Lord, when the reaper will be overtaken by the ploughman and the planter by the one treading grapes*" (Amos 9:13).

**k) No Unemployment:**   "*They will rebuild the ancient ruins and restore the places long devastated; they will renew the ruined cities that have been devasated for generations*" (Isa.61:4).

**l) There will be Domestic Security:** "*Every man will sit under his own vine and under his own fig-tree, and no-one will make them afraid, for the Lord Almighty has spoken* " (Micah 4:4).

**m) A Sound Education System:** "*.......He will teach us of his ways....The Law will go out from Zion, the word of the Lord from Jerusalem* " (Isa.2:3).

**n) New Social Standards:**   "*The fruit of righteousness will be peace, the effect of righteousness will be  quietness and confidence for ever* " (Isa. 32:17).

**o) God's Will Established on the Earth:** "*Your kingdom come, your will be done on earth as it is in heaven*" (Matt.6:10).

**Notes:**

1. Churchill, Sir Winston. *His Complete Speeches*, edited by Robert R. James, Volume vii, p.7488.

# Chapter 19

---

# The Millennial Temple

Since the early days of Moses, the central focus for the worship of God's people was the relocatable Tabernacle. During the Kingdom period of history, King David and the people desired to build a permanent dwelling place of worship. Although David was not permitted to build the Temple, his son Solomon did. That masterpiece of construction from God's drawing board stood until the fall of the Southern Kingdom by Nebuchadnezzar in 586 B.C.

After the 70 years of Jewish captivity in Babylon, Zerubbabel built another less glorious Temple. Over the years this smaller Temple deteriorated, so when Herod The Great arrived on the scene he virtually demolished the structure and built a very much enlarged architectural wonder that took at least 46 years to complete (Jn.2:20). It stood in golden splendour above the skyline of Jerusalem. It was to this Temple that Jesus was presented as an eight day old baby (Lk.2:21), and where He astounded the Jewish authorities with His wisdom at the age of twelve years(Lk.2:47).

With the destruction of this Temple by Titus

the Roman general in 70 A.D, and the subsequent dispersion of the Jews to all parts of the globe; Temple sacrifices stopped. However, there has always been a deep yearning within the Jew - for a place on Mount Moriah in which he could once again worship God through the sacrificial system.

**Two Temples Remain to be Built in Jerusalem**

The prophecies of the Bible reveal that this earnest desire by the religious Jews to build a Temple will be fulfilled in the future. One will be constructed just prior to or during the early days of the Tribulation Period. This is the Temple spoken of by Daniel the prophet, and will be built in unbelief.  According to Daniel, because of the Jewish authorities almost fanatical desire to reintroduce the sacrificial system, God will allow the Antichrist to occupy this Temple at the mid-Tribulation point, thus bringing to a halt any worship by the Jews in their beloved Temple.

This Temple is referred to as the **"Tribulation Temple."**

The final Temple to be built on this earth will be known as the **"Millennial Temple."** It will be the most glorious and vast structure of any of its predecessors. In fact, it will outshine any church presently standing today. It will be built in the holy city of Jerusalem during the 1000 year reign of Jesus Christ. The prophets Isaiah, Ezekiel, and Micah gave many details concerning this Temple from which Christ will physically rule the earth.

Through the prophet Ezekiel the Lord said,

*"This will be the place of my throne, and the place for the soles of my feet. This is where I will live among the Israelites forever"* (Ezek.43:7).

## The Dimensions of the Temple

The size of the structure to be built during the Millennium almost defies imagination. The blueprint and operation manual is detailed in Ezekiel chapters 40 to 48.

It will tower above the skyline of the city in the rising sun, golden in splendour, glistening in beauty. At dawn or sunset, noon or night, the Temple will be the focal point of Jerusalem. It will be the place where God dwells among His people.

Ezekiel chapters 40 to 42 give detailed measurements of this building. The specifications record dimensions of the porches, gates, rooms, and the thickness of the walls, and outlines how it will all fit together. A summary of these measurements is recorded in chapter 42:15-20.

The Temple area itself will measure approximately 250 meters square. It will be the largest and most magnificent structure ever erected, and it will be dedicated to the glory of God.

## Topographical Changes will take place

This Temple, together with its accompanying outer precincts will necessitate significant changes to the land formation around present-day Jerusalem. This change is predicted by the prophets:
*"In the last days the mountain of the Lord's temple*

*will be established as chief among the mountains; It will be raised above the hills, and people will stream to it. Many nations will come and say, Let us go up to the mountain of the Lord and to the house of the God of Jacob"* (Micah 4:1-2).

*"In the last days the mountain of the Lord's temple will be established as chief among the mountains. It will be raised above the hills, and all nations will stream to it "* (Isa.2:2).

*"For on my holy mountain, the high mountain of Israel, declares the sovereign Lord, there in the land the entire house of Israel will serve me...."* (Ezek.20:40).

These great changes will all come about when Jesus Christ touches down on the Mount of Olives, as recorded in Zechariah chapter 14. The Mount of Olives will split into two parts and a fountain of living water will flow towards the Mediterranean and also towards the Dead Sea. We are further told that Jerusalem will be raised considerably higher than its present 800 meters above sea level.

Not only will Jerusalem be raised up as a high mountain, but it will be greatly enlarged as well. Ezekiel 45:1 indicates that the holy portion only of the land will be immense, measuring some 12 kilometers by10 kilometres, which is equal to 120 square kilometres. This is considerably larger than present day old and new Jerusalem combined.

The chapter continues to detail further measurements relating to other areas allocated to the priests and Levites. As we ponder all this, we get a better picture of just how big our God is.

## The Glory of God Returns to His Temple

The  saddest day in the history of Jewish worship was when the "Shekinah Glory"- that all-consuming invisible presence of God, reluctantly in a series of movements - departed (*Ichabod*) from the Temple just before the nation of Israel went into captivity as a judgment for her sins. This sad event is recorded in Ezekiel chapter 10.

Now the scene had changed. Ezekiel was privileged to look far beyond his days to see the Glory of the Lord returning through the eastern gate, returning to the new Temple to dwell in the inner court (Ezek.43:2-5).  This description corresponds to John's account of the return of Jesus Christ as recorded in the Book of Revelation (1:15).

The presence of the Lord will return to a Jewish Temple in Jerusalem and will remain for 1000 years.

## The Priesthood in the Millennial Temple

The Scriptures are very clear as to who will have the responsibility of ministering in God's Holy Millennial Temple: "*But the priests who are Levites and decendants of Zadok and who faithfully carried out the duties of my sanctuary when the Israelites went astray from me, are to come near to minister before me; they are to stand before me to offer sacrifices of fat and blood, declares the  Sovereign Lord. They alone are to enter my sanctuary; they alone are to come near my table to minister before me and perform my service*" (Ezek.44:15-16).

## The Sons of Zodak

The designation of the decendants of Zadok as the priests of the Temple (see also Ezek.40:46; 43:19; 48:11) provides us with two items of helpful information:

**1.** It proves the literalness of the future Millennial Temple, simply because real names are documented.

**2.** It once again supports the theology that God will faithfully reward those who in turn are faithful to Him in Christian service.

## Sacrifices in the Millennial Temple. Why?

Ezekiel chapters 40-48 clearly state that sacrifices will be offered in this magnificent Temple This invokes the age old question. **Why?** Doesn't the Book of Hebrews teach that the sacrificial atoning death of Christ was once and for all and totally sufficient?

The future sacrifices are ones to be carried out in the Temple of God on this earth only during the Millennium. (Note: In the Eternal state death is eliminated and sacrifices will not be practised).

The sacrifices will  be memorial ones to the work of Christ on the cross. They will in no way detract from the redeeming work at Calvary. They will be no more redemptive than the sacrifices offered before Calvary.

The church celebrates the Lord's Supper as a memorial of His death. This does not detract from the cross, but serves as a constant reminder of what Christ did for us. Just as the Lord's Supper is not a detraction, neither will be the Millennial Sacrifices.

# Chapter 20

# The Clean-up
# Before
# Eternity

During the Millennial Reign of Jesus Christ conditions on earth will not be perfect, but could be best described as "ideal." Satan will be bound, and therefore will not have any influence over the inhabitants of the earth.

These inhabitants will be people in their fleshly bodies who have survived the Great Tribulation and did not take the "Mark of the Beast." Sin and death will be greatly reduced, but will not as yet be eliminated. Flesh will always be contaminated with sin, no matter how good a life a person may try to live. Scripture gives evidence to the fact that there will be death during the Millennium (Isa.65:20). This will probably occur where there is out and out rebellion against the Reign of Christ.

It is at the conclusion of this one thousand years of ideal conditions and environment on earth that mankind must face one final test. To qualify for entry into the Eternal State, all those who entered the Millennium in their fleshly bodies, together with all the people born during the one thousand years, must make a decision as to whether they wish to follow Christ or Satan.

# The Release of Satan

*"When the thousand years are over, Satan will be released from his prison and will go out to deceive the nations in the four corners of the earth - Gog and Magog - to gather them for battle. In number they are like the sands of the seashore. They marched across the breadth of the earth and surrounded the camp of God's people, the city he loves. But fire came down from Heaven and devoured them. And the devil who deceived them was thrown into the lake of burning sulphur, where the beast and the false prophet had been thrown. They will be tormented day and night for ever and ever "* (Rev 20:7-10).

By the time Satan is released there will be a great number of unbelievers, people who reject the firm direction from the saints and the governmental control of Jesus Christ.

The extent of the deception from Satan is revealed in the expression Gog and Magog, which indicates that Satan's activities will reach to all corners of the earth. The similarity to this battle and the one recorded in Ezekiel is demonstrated by the massive invasion of Jerusalem this time, Millennial Jerusalem. However, the invading forces will be quickly dispensed with by fire out of heaven, destroying them with lighting speed (v.9).

At this point the instigator of the revolt is thrown into his final and eternal abode - the lake of burning sulphur. Satan will never be active again.

# The Great White Throne Judgment

This will be the last and final judgment mankind will have to face. It is a judgment to eternal death for all the unsaved sinners. It takes place after the Millennium, but before the establishment of the Eternal Order.

The purpose of the judgment will not be to determine whether a person is saved or not, for that issue was settled when the unsaved died. They will be raised from "death and Hades" to stand in their fleshly bodies before the righteous Judge Jesus Christ, the One to Whom authority has been given to judge (Jn.5:22).

## God's Books are Opened

God has four (4) diaries from which He records information on the life of mankind:

**1. The Book of Life** (Rev.20:15;  Rev.3:5)

When a person is born, his name enters the book of life. This book contains the names of all living people. When that person dies without accepting Christ, his name is removed from the book of life.

- **2. The Lamb's Book of Life** (Rev.21:27)

When a person calls on the Lamb for salvation, his name remains in the book of life, but is duplicated into the Lamb's book of life.

**3. The Book of Man's Works** (Rev.20:12-13)

All mankind who have rejected Jesus Christ will stand before the Great White Throne judgment. When the book of Life is opened, it will be found to be empty, and so all the people in this category will be judged out of the Book of Man's Works.

*"And I saw the dead, great and small, standing before the throne, and* **books** *were opened. Another book was opened, which is the book of life. The dead were judged according to what they had done as recorded in the books...."* (Rev.20:12).

### 4. The Book of the Law  (Gal.3:10)

All the Old Testament people who did not keep the Law of Moses and thereby rejected Jehovah, will be judged out of this book as well as the book of man's works.

### What will be the Verdict?

Scripture is very clear on this issue. **Guilty!** The destiny for the person appearing at this judgment is not some place where reformation can take place. It will not be a huge compound where all the "baddies" can have a good time as some would like to suggest. No! The word of God says, *"If anyone's name was  not found written in the book of Life, he was thrown into the lake of fire "* (Rev. 20:15).

Hell is the place of torment for the souls of all non-believers waiting the judgment at the Great White Throne. At the time of the Second Resurrection the bodies of the unsaved from the grave will be united with their souls from Hell.The lake of fire is the eternal destiny of both soul and body. God has done everything possible to save the sinner from a lost eternity,  but it is because God is holy and righteous that He must punish the sinner.

# Chapter 21

# The Eternal Kingdom of God the Father

The last two chapters of the Bible give the only reference to what the believer can anticipate in the Eternal State. A new dimention is now introduced. Jesus Christ - the Son - hands back the Reign to the Father. The Holy City, the New Jerusalem, is the dwelling place of God. From this point onwards the Father will be with men, and He will dwell with them (Rev.12:3).

There will be no more death, mourning, crying or pain. God's presence will bring perfect peace and joy, for the old order of things has passed away (v.4).

There are five **(5)** <u>new concepts</u> introduced in chapters 21 and 22 of Revelation:

1. **A New Heaven and New Earth;**
2. **The New Jerusalem;**
3. **A New Paradise;**
4. **A New Form of Humanity;**
5. **A New Vocation.**

# 1. A New Heaven and New Earth

The term "new heavens and new earth" is found in an earlier book in the New Testament. The apostle Peter says,"*But in keeping with his promise we are looking forward to a new heaven and a new earth, the home of righteousness*" (2 Pet.3:13). The present earth and heavens are said to be "*reserved for fire until the day of judgment*" (v.7).

In second Peter, the new heavens and earth appear after "*the elements melt with fervent heat*" (v.10). It is therefore quite conclusive that the "new heavens and new earth" appear after the Millennial Reign of Jesus Christ, and the Great White Throne judgment.

This term "new heaven(s) and new earth" is found in only two other places in the Bible. In Isaiah 65:17-18 we read, "*Behold, I will create new heavens and a new earth. The former things will not be remembered, nor will they come to mind. But be glad and rejoice forever in what I will create.*"

Isaiah 66:22 says, "*As the new heavens and the new earth that I will make will endure before me, declares the Lord, so will your name and decendants endure.*"

In both references we are given to understand that our new dwelling place will be one that will endure without any reference to time. It will be a place of permanency.

## Why would God want to destroy the Heavens?

It is understandable that God would destroy the earth, but why "the heaven" (22:1)? The answer is quite simple. The atmospheric heavens are contaminated with evil.

Note: There are three **(3)** heavens.
   **a)** The atmospheric heaven around the earth;
   **b)** The stellar heaven containing the galaxies;
   **c)** The third heaven, or the throne of God.
   It is this atmospheric heaven which has been the abode of Satan (Eph.6:12; Job1:7).

The Holy City, which our Lord went to prepare for His saints (Jn.14:1-3), will come down from heaven to this new earth. No longer will God's Tabernacle be in the third heaven. He will move His headquarters to the new earth, which is the saints' Eternal home, and will take up His abode in the New Jerusalem. With our present mental capacity and limited understanding, we have difficulty comprehending the full significance of one day living in God's front garden.

## 2. The New Jerusalem

There have been a number of differing opinions as to what this concept means. Some scholars say that it represents a real city. Others claim it is only an allegory of the perfected and Eternal church. Careful reading of the passage will soon reveal that the Bible presents a clear vision of the New

Jerusalem as a literal, actual city of incredible dimensions and splendor.

This Holy City is a city located in the sky, and is described as a 1500 miles (2400 kms.) cube (Rev.21:16). Its walls are of pure gold; its foundations are of pure stones; its streets are transparent. More importantly, this city has no Temple. The city has no light bearers. The very presence of God within gives it light. *"The nations will walk by its light, and the kings of the earth will bring their splendor into it"* (Rev.21:24).

## Characteristics of the New Jerusalem

**1.** The new Jerusalem comes to a new earth, for the old one has passed away (Rev.21:1-2).
**2.** The city has a great high wall with 12 gates. These contain the names of the 12 tribes of Israel (v.12).
**3.** The city has 12 foundations with the names of the 12 apostles (v.14).
**4.** The foundations of the city walls are decorated with 12 precious stones (vv.18-20).
**5.** Each city gate is formed from one single incredible pearl (v.21).
**6.** The city streets are made of pure gold, giving them a transparent appearance (v.21).
**7.** This city had no Temple because God and the Lamb are its Temple (v.22).
**8.** There is no night in the city. The city needs no sun or moon. God and the Lamb illuminate it (vv.23,25).
**9.** Nothing impure will ever enter this city. Only those whose names are written in the Lamb's Book of Life can enter it (v.27).

## 3. A New Paradise

The first five verses of Chapter 22 emphasize a special and beautiful part of the New Jerusalem. John paints for us a picture of "*the river of the water of life, clear as crystal, flowing from the throne of God and of the Lamb, right through the centre of the city*" (vv.1-2).

Along the river, on each side, John sees the "Tree of Life" fully laden with fruit and whose leaves "*are for the healing of the nations*" (v.2). There is no curse, no darkness - all a product of sin. There will be personal access to God, and we will reign for ever and ever (22:5).

The "Tree of Life" symbol is first introduced at the beginning of the Book of Genesis. In chapter 3:24, mankind, who previously had direct access to the Tree of Life was barred from any contact with that tree which stood as a symbol of the gift of Eternal life. Adam had sinned, thereby disobeying his Maker, and as a consequence he had spiritually disqualified himself.

Today nothing has changed. Mankind continues to sin and therefore is barred from access to the "Tree of Life." In the Book of Revelation we see that salvation is offered to all who are willing to be obedient to God's commands and accept His Son Jesus as their personal Saviour and Redeemer. The way to the "Tree of Life" is no longer blocked to the believer. Repentant humans from all nations are able to enter into a relationship of love and obedience with their Maker. This is the clear teaching of Revelation chapter 22.

## 4. A New Form of Humanity

Very little is revealed about life in our new surroundings, except that nations and kings will exist. What will it be like co-existing with angels? The scene is certainly far removed from our present weak situation. Our new bodies will be characterized by power, and they will be controlled by the spiritual rather than subject to the physical.

Perhaps the scene in the upper room may give us a small clue. Christ appeared to His disciples through a locked room. He ate with them, although He was uniquely flesh and bone. He was totally recognizable, but yet was different (Lk.24). What an expectation!

## 5. A New Vocation

God created the Garden of Eden, then created Adam and Eve to share in His creation. Did God then say, "Sit back Adam and Eve and relax for all Eternity"? No! Adam was told to work and take care of the garden (Gen.2:15).

We are not privy to all the plans of God during the Eternal State, nor has God revealed the activities that will occupy the time in our new dwelling. But we can be sure of one thing, and it is this: such an active and creative God would not shape Eternity for a passive existence. Whatever our state of existence may be, it will certainly be delightful in the Eternal presence of the One Who redeemed us from

Planet Earth.

Thus Revelation completes the circle and heals the breach between man and God, a breach which started with Adam shortly after creation. It closes the chapter on humanity's walk towards death.

It is appropiate to close this book with a challenge from one of the greatest Old Testament men, the  prophet and lawgiver Moses:

*"See, I set before you today life and prosperity, death and destruction. For I command you today to love the Lord your God, to walk in his ways, and to keep his commands, decrees and laws, then you will live and increase, and the Lord your God will bless you in the land you are entering to possess...... This day I call heaven and earth as witness against you that I have set before you life and death, blessings and curses. Now choose life...."* (Deut.30:15-16,19).

**May God give us grace to respond to the challengers of His Holy Word.**

**Amen.**

# BIBLIOGRAPHY

Anderson, Robert. *The Coming Prince.* London: Hodder & Stoughton, Reprinted 1985.

Chapman, Colin. *Whose Promised Land?* London: Lion Publishing Company, 1983.

Clouse, G. Robert. *The Meaning of the Millennium-four views.* Illinois: Inter Varsity Press, 1977.

Chacour, Elais. *Blood Brothers.* Sussex, Great Britian: Kingsway Publications Ltd, 1986.

Davidson, Elishua. *Islam, Israel, and the Last Days.* Oregon, USA: Harvest House Publishers, 1991.

Davis & Whitcomb. *A History of Israel.* Grand Rapids, MI: Baker Book House, 1980.

Douglas & Tenney. *The New International Dictionary of the Bible.* Hants,UK: Marshall Pickering Publishers, 1987.

Dyer, Charles. *The Rise of Babylon.* Wheaton, Illinois: Tyndale House Publishers, Inc, 1991.

Friederichsen, Paul. *Prophecy Unveiled- Revelation Smplified.* California, USA. Evangelistic Literature Ent, 1989.

Fruchtenbaum, Arnold. *The Footsteps of the Messiah.* California: Ariel Press, 1984.

Fausset, A.R. *Bible Encyclopedia and Dictionary - Critical & Expository.* Grand Rapids, MI: Zondervan, undated.

Geisler, Norman. *A Popular Survey of the Old Testament.* Grand Rapids, MI: Baker Book House, 1977.

Halley, H. Henry. *Halley's Bible Handbook.* Grand Rapids, MI: Zondervan Publishing House, 24th Ed., 1965.

Ironside, H.A. *Lectures on Daniel the Prophet.* New York: Loizeaux Brothers, 1986.

Keil,C.F. & Delitzsch, F. *Commentary on the Old Testament.* Grand Rapids, MI: W.B. Eerdmans Publishing, 1951.

LaHaye,Tim. *Revelation.* Grand Rapids, MI: Zondervan, 1979.

--------. *The beginning of the End.* Wheaton, Illinois: Tyndale House Publishers, 1981.

--------. *Life in the Afterlife,* Wheaton, Illinois: Tyndale, 1980.

Lindsay, Hal. *There's A New World Coming.* California: Vision House Publishers, 1973.

--------, *The Late Great Planet Earth.* Melbourne, Australia: S.John Bacon, 1970.

Levy, David. Joel - The Day of the Lord. New Jersey, USA: The Friends of Israel Gospel Ministry, Inc., 1987.

Marrs, Texe. *Dark Secrets of the New Age*. Westchester, Illinois: Crossway Books, 1987.

New Bible Dictionary, 2nd. Ed. Wheaton, Illinois, USA: Tyndale House, 1982.

Packer, Merrill, Tenney, White. *All the People and Places of the Bible*. Nashville Tn: Thomas Nelson Inc., 1982.

Payne, J. Barton. *Encyclopedia of Bible Prophecy*. Grand Rapids, MI: Baker Book House, 1973.

Pentecost, J. Dwight. *Things to come*. Grand Rapids, MI: Zondervan Publishing House, 1958.

Scott, Walter. *Exposition of the Revelation of Jesus Christ.* London: Pickering & Inglis Ltd. 4th Ed. undated.

Scofield, C.I. Scofield Bible Correspondance Course. Vol.3. Chicago, Illinois, USA: Moody Bible Institute, 1907.

Tatford, F.A. *The Final Battle*. Great Britain: New Wine Press, 1987.

Tozer, A.W. *The Coming King*. Great Britain: Kingsway Publication, 1990.

The Lion Handbook to the Bible. Herts, G.B: Lion Pub. 1981.

The Illustrated Bible Dictionary. Parts 1,2,3. Leicester, G.B: Inter-Varsity Press, 1980.

The World Book Encyclopedia. USA: Field Enterprises Corporation, 1974.

Unger, F. Merrill. *The New Unger's Bible Handbook*. Chicago: Moody Press, 1984.

Walvoord, F. John. *Daniel, the Key to Prophetic Revelation.* Chicago, Illinois: Moody Press, 1971

-------. *The Revelation of Jesus Christ: A Commentary.* Chicago, Illinois: Moody Press,1966.

Wood, Leon. *A commentary on Daniel.* Grand rapids, MI: Zondervan Publishing House, 1973.

Willmington, H.L. *The King is Coming*. Wheaton, Illinois: Tyndale House Publishers, 1983.

Yerbury, W. Ray. *Prophecies of Daniel.* Brisbane, Australia: Cross Publications, 1988.

-------. *The Ultimate Event - A Bible Study in Prophecy.* Brisbane, Australia: Cross Publications, 1988.

-------. *Vital Signs of Christ's Coming.* Brisbane, Australia: Cross Publications, 1990.

Other books by Dr. Ray Yerbury:

**PROPHECIES OF DANIEL**
**THE ULTIMATE EVENT**
**VITAL SIGNS OF CHRIST'S COMING**

**NOTES**

 **NOTES**